WHEN A SPOUSE DIES
A STEP-BY-STEP GUIDE
TO WHAT COMES NEXT
patricia a. farrell, ph.d.
author of
"how to be your
own
therapist"

Amazon author page for https://tinyurl.com/yc3vff2n

In the Fired by the Future Series

Book One: You Just Lost Your Job. You Are Not Broken.

How to Stop the Spiral, Find Your Footing, and Take Your First Step in the New Economy

Book Two: The Skills That Cannot Be Fired.

How to Find, Build, and Sell the Human Abilities That AI and Automation Will Never Replace

Book Three: The Trades Are Hiring. Are You Ready? (This book)

The No-Nonsense Guide to Landing a High-Paying Trade Job Without a Four-Year Degree

Book Four: Your Second Act.

Building Income the New Economy Cannot Take Away

PATRICIA A. FARRELL, PH.D.

The Pocket Companion Series contains:

When Your Mind Won't Stop

After the Loss: Finding Your Way Through Grief

You Are Enough: Rebuilding Your Self-Worth

At the Crossroads: Making Decisions When Nothing Feels Clear

When People Hurt: Navigating Difficult Relationships

When You Feel Stuck: Finding Movement in Hard Times

Books by Patricia A. Farrell, Ph.D.

Better Together, Book 3: Reasons we heal

The Belief Effect, Book 2: Reasons we heal

Wired for Good, Book 1: Reasons we heal

Get Out! A shrink's guide to using the great outdoors for therapy

When You Can't Pour From an Empty Glass: CBT Skills for Exhausted Caregivers

The Little Book on Learning Big Critical Thinking Skills

The Smart Kid's Survival Guide: Making Good Choices in a Confusing World

How to Be Your Own Therapist

It's Not All in Your Head: Anxiety, Depression, Mood Swings and Multiple Sclerosis

Unfiltered: Beneath the noise of our thoughts lies the true narrative of our minds

Unfiltered Again: A behind-the-scenes look at healthcare, medicine and mental health

A Social Security Disability Psychological Claims Handbook: A simple guide to understanding your SSD claim for psychological impairments and unraveling the maze of decision-making

A Social Security Disability Psychological Claims Guidebook for Children's Benefits

The Disability Accessible US Parks in All 50 States: A Comprehensive Guide

Birding in the US NOW!: A birding guide for individuals with disabilities

Contents

A Note Before You Begin

This book is for you if your husband or wife or partner just died and you are the one left to handle everything. It is written especially for you if you live with a disability that makes some of these steps harder. It is also written for you if you don't have children to call for help.

You do not have to read this book in order. You do not have to read it in one sitting. Some chapters cover the first few days. Others cover things that will not matter to you for weeks or months. *Skip around.* Come back later. Put the book down when it is too much and pick it up again when you are ready. You decide everything from now on, and this book is meant to guide you in the most gentle manner possible. There is no stress, and you don't have to do anything until you feel up to it or until you can get the appropriate assistance that you need with something. There will be days when you won't want to do anything, and that's okay. It's to be expected. There will be other days when you will want to work through things quickly, and that's all right too. There is no wrong way to do anything here, but there are things that you will have to attend to. I know many days won't be easy.

Here is why this book is different from a lot of what you will find. It does not use legal words or financial words without explaining them first. It breaks big, scary jobs into small steps you can actually do. It was written with the idea that you might be tired, in pain, grieving, and doing all of this alone. Nothing in here assumes you have a grown child who can drive you somewhere or sit on hold with an insurance company for you.

You have permission to go slow. You have permission to ask for help. You have permission to feel behind, because there is no such thing as behind here. There is only the next right step, whenever you are ready to take it.

How to Use This Book

The book is broken into six parts. **Part One** covers the first days after your beloved died. **Part Two** covers the first thirty days. **Part Three** explains legal matters like wills and property. **Part Four** is about building a stable financial life on your own. Part Five is about daily life and getting help when you do not have family nearby. Part Six is about grief and about you, not just the paperwork.

Many chapters include a checklist. Use it. Cross things off as you go, even small things. Seeing a list get shorter is proof that you are moving forward, even on days when it doesn't feel like it.

Some chapters include a short story about a hypothetical person. These are not real people. Each story blends small pieces from many different situations, and enough details are changed—names, ages, towns, jobs, and exact events—so that no single person could be recognized. The point of these stories is to show you that other people have stood where you are standing now and to make a step in the chapter feel real instead of just being a rule on a page.

In the back of the book, you will find a few checklists, a resource directory organized by topic, and a glossary of the confusing words you will run into along the way.

Why this book uses plain language on purpose

You will notice that this book explains every term the first time it comes up, even ones you might already know. That is intentional. *Grief makes it harder to hold new information in your head, even information you would normally understand without trouble.* Plain language isn't written for people who can't understand complicated language. It is written so that nobody has to spend extra energy translating a word before they can use the information behind it. You have better things to spend your energy on right now.

You will also notice this book avoids comparing your loss to a storm, a journey, a wound that heals, or anything else. *Those comparisons are common in books about grief,* and some readers find them comforting. *This book sticks to plain, direct description instead,* because the goal here is usefulness, not poetry. If you want that kind of writing, there are wonderful books built around it, but this simply is not one of them.

If you are reading this for someone else

Maybe you are not the widow, widower, or bereaved yourself. Maybe you are a friend, a neighbor, an adult niece or nephew, or a home care aide who picked this book up to help someone you care about. Everything in this book still applies. Read a chapter together, or read ahead and bring back the parts most likely to matter this week. Being the second set of eyes on this process is *one of the most useful things you can offer someone right now,* even if you cannot solve the grief itself.

PART 1: The First Days

This part covers *the first day through the first week*. It only *covers what truly needs to happen right now*. Everything else can wait. You will find guidance here in the first few hours, on the words you are about to hear from funeral homes and government offices, and on the practical decisions around a funeral, burial, or cremation that tend to arrive faster than anyone feels ready for. *Nothing in this part requires a decision you cannot take back*, and nothing here requires you to have figured out the rest of your life yet. It is only about getting through these first several days as gently as the circumstances allow.

Chapter 1: When the Phone Rings

Your spouse or partner has died. Maybe it happened at home. Maybe it happened in a hospital, or in an ambulance, or somewhere else. However it happened, you are now facing a list of things that feel urgent, and most of them are not. In this moment, you may be wondering what you should do first and who you should contact. You are not even sure how you feel. You may be shocked, panic-stricken, or almost riveted in place, feeling unable to do anything. Believe me, you can do what is required, and there are people who are waiting to help you.

Here is the truth that almost nobody tells you in the first hour: ***very little has to happen right away***. You do not have to plan a funeral tonight. You do not have to call everyone you know tonight. You do not have to decide anything permanent tonight. Your only job right now is to get through the next few hours.

What actually has to happen now

If your spouse died at home and was not already under hospice care, call 911. Tell the dispatcher your spouse has died. They will send someone to confirm it and guide you through the next step, which is usually contacting a funeral home or the coroner's office.

If your spouse was under hospice care, call the hospice nurse line first, not 911. Hospice has a nurse on call day and night for exactly this moment. They will come to the house, confirm the death, and call the funeral home for you. This is one of the most useful things hospice does, and it is worth knowing ahead of time if your spouse is currently in hospice care.

If your spouse died in a hospital, the staff will handle the immediate steps and will ask you which funeral home you want to use.

Once the death is confirmed, you need to choose a funeral home if you have not already chosen one. If you already had a plan in place, whether through a funeral home, a cremation society, or a prepaid plan, call that number. If you do not have a plan, it is fine to pick one now. *You are not locked into anything permanent by making this first call.* **Chapter 3** walks through funeral, burial, and cremation choices in detail, including specific costs, so you do not have to figure that out in the first hour.

Who to call first

After the funeral home or hospice, call the people closest to you. This usually means your closest family member, your closest friend, and anyone who lives nearby and can come sit with you. You do not need to call everyone tonight. You need one or two people who can be physically present with you or on the phone with you.

If you live with a disability and rely on your spouse for physical tasks, daily routines, or transportation, this is also the moment to *think about who can step in for the next few days.* A neighbor, a friend from church, or a home care agency if you already use one. **Chapter 3** has more on asking for this kind of help in the first week.

If your spouse died away from home

If your spouse died while traveling, in another state, or somewhere far from your local funeral home, there is an added step: getting your spouse's body transported home, if that is what you want. A funeral home in the place of death can typically arrange this transport, working together with a funeral home near you to handle the receiving end. This adds cost and time, so *ask both funeral homes for a combined, written estimate before agreeing to anything,* and ask specifically what the transport fee includes. One good question to always ask, in almost any situation, *is, "Is there anything else I should know that I haven't asked*?"

If your spouse died outside the country, the process involves the nearest United States embassy or consulate, which can help arrange the paperwork needed to bring your spouse's body or cremated remains home. This is a slower process, *often taking one to two weeks*, and it is worth knowing that in advance so the wait does not feel like something has gone wrong.

When there is no plan already in place

If your spouse did not leave any written wishes and had no prepaid plan, you are the one making these decisions, possibly for the first time, while exhausted and in shock. This is common, not a failure to plan ahead. Funeral home staff handle this conversation daily and are generally trained to walk you through the basic decisions gently, one at a time, rather than all at once. If a particular funeral home's staff feels rushed, pushy, or hard to understand, you are allowed to call a different one instead. You are not required to use the first place you call. When my mother died from metastatic cancer after being in hospice, we knew we would have to make arrangements even before she had passed. With that thought in mind, my sister and I visited three funeral homes in the area and received all of the particulars from each of them. We then made a choice and the agreement that was required. Fortunately, we did have time on our side.

If you have a mobility limitation or physical disability yourself

If your spouse was the one who helped you get in and out of bed, in and out of the shower, up from a chair, or around the house safely, their death is not only an emotional loss. It is also the sudden loss of your physical support system, on top of everything else happening this week. This deserves direct, practical attention in the first few days, not just quiet endurance.

If you are not safe managing alone right now, even for a night or two, say so plainly to whoever is helping you: a family member, a neighbor, or a home care agency if you already use one. "*I cannot safely get into the shower alone tonight*" or "*I need someone here in the mornings until I figure out a longer-term plan*" are reasonable, specific things to say out loud. If no one close to you can help immediately, call your Area Agency on Aging, covered fully in **Chapter 16**, and explain that you have lost your in-home support unexpectedly. Many areas have emergency or short-term home care options for exactly this kind of situation, and a caseworker can often arrange something within a day or two rather than the weeks a standard intake might normally take.

If you already had paid home care or a visiting nurse in place before your spouse died, that arrangement almost certainly continues unaffected. If your spouse was your only support and you had nothing paid or formal in place, treat setting that up as one of the most urgent tasks in this entire book, ahead of most of the paperwork covered in the chapters that follow. **Chapter 16** walks through how to find and afford this kind of help in more detail once the first few days have passed.

Taking care of pets and immediate household needs

If your spouse was the one who normally fed a pet, took a pet out, or handled another small daily household task, arrange for someone, a neighbor, a family member, or a pet-sitting service, to cover it for the next several days while your attention is elsewhere. This is a small, practical thing, but it is one less thing pulling at you during a week when your attention is already stretched thin.

What can wait a few days

Here is a short list of things that *do not need to happen tonight or even tomorrow*:

1. Notifying every friend and distant relative. Word travels. Let it travel at its own pace, or ask one person to help spread the word for you.

2. Canceling accounts, subscriptions, or memberships. None of these are going anywhere in the next few days.

3. Deciding what to do with your spouse's belongings. This can wait weeks or months. There is no deadline.

4. Making any decision about your house, your car, or where you will live. Big decisions made in the first few days, while you are in shock, are rarely good ones. Give yourself time.

5. Applying for survivor benefits. You will get to this in the coming weeks. It is covered fully in **Chapter 5.**

A short list of things not to sign or decide yet

1. In the first day or two, you may be handed paperwork by a funeral home, a hospital, or even someone claiming to represent an insurance company. *Slow down before you sign anything beyond the basic paperwork needed* to release your spouse's body and begin funeral arrangements.

2. Do not sign any contract for funeral services you have not had time to read, especially one with a total cost you have not seen in writing. All contracts should be very specific about

what will be done and what the cost will be for each. Enumerated items like this are needed because, in their absence, you may be paying for things you never wanted or cannot afford. Unfortunately, this is a time when some will use grief as a means to profit, and you do not want to be victimized like that.

3. Do not agree to any purchase over the phone from someone who contacted you first, even if they claim to be with a benefits office or an insurance company. Legitimate agencies do not pressure you to decide immediately. **Chapter 10** covers this kind of scam in detail.

4. Do not sign anything related to your spouse's estate, property, or accounts until you have had a chance to **read Chapters 8 and 9**.

5. If someone is rushing you to sign something in the first day or two, it is reasonable to say *you need more time,* even if that feels uncomfortable. A death in the family does not create a deadline that overrides your right to read something before you sign it.

One Woman's Story

In the middle of the night after her husband died at home, a woman we will call Ruth sat at her kitchen table with a phone in her hand and no idea who to call first. Her husband had been sick for months, but the end still came faster than she expected. She called 911 out of habit, and the dispatcher walked her through what would happen next, gently, one step at a time.

A deputy coroner came to the house. He was kind and unhurried. He asked if she had a funeral home in mind, and when she said no, he gave her a list and waited while she made a call. It was almost four in the morning before the house was quiet again. Ruth said later that the thing *she wished she had known was that she did not have to decide anything else that night.* She thought she had to plan a funeral before sunrise. She did not. She went to bed, and the world didn't fall apart because she waited until morning to do the next thing.

Chapter 2: Words You Will Start Hearing

Over the next few weeks, you are going to hear words that funeral homes, banks, and government offices use every day but that most people never had a reason to learn. This chapter *defines the most important ones* in plain language, so that when you hear them later in the book, or from a stranger on the phone, you already know what they mean. Anything you don't understand can be questioned. You are allowed to ask any questions you wish in order to fully understand what someone is proposing or telling you. You are not a child, and you should not be treated like one. You deserve respect.

Executor. The person named in a will, or appointed by a court if there is no will, who is responsible for handling the deceased person's estate. This includes paying debts, filing paperwork, and distributing what is left to the people who inherit it. If your spouse named you as executor, this job will fall to you.

Probate. The court process that legally settles a person's estate after death. Probate confirms the will is valid, if there is one, and gives the executor the legal authority to act. Not everything has to go through probate. **Chapter 8** explains what does and does not. *If the estate is small, the will is not being challenged, and the family agrees on how to divide the assets,* an executor can typically complete the probate paperwork and court filings ***without the services of a lawyer.*** However, some states or complicated cases do necessitate an attorney.

Beneficiary. A person named to receive money or property from an account, policy, or will. Life insurance policies, retirement accounts, and bank accounts often let the owner name a beneficiary directly, which means that money can go to that person *without going through probate at all.*

Next of kin. The closest living relative. This term is mostly used by hospitals, funeral homes, and some government forms to figure out who has the legal right to make decisions when there is no other paperwork in place.

Power of attorney. A legal document that lets one person make decisions for another person. **There are different kinds,** some for financial decisions and some for health care decisions. Once your spouse has died, any power of attorney they held for you, or that you held for them, ends. **Chapter 7 and Chapter 11** explain what to do next if you relied on this kind of document.

Death certificate. The official document proving a death occurred, including the cause and date. *You will need certified copies* of this document for almost every step in this book, from claiming benefits to closing accounts. **Chapter 3** explains exactly how many to get and what they cost.

Estate. Everything a person owned at the time of death: money, property, belongings, and debts. The estate is what gets settled through probate or handled outside of it, depending on how accounts and property were set up.

Joint tenancy and survivorship. Terms that describe *property owned by two people together,* usually a house or a bank account, where the surviving owner automatically becomes the sole owner when the other person dies. **Chapter 9** explains how this works for your home specifically.

Intestate. The legal term for *dying without a valid will.* **Chapter 8** explains what happens to property when this is the case and why it matters more when there are no children.

Letters testamentary. The document *a probate court gives the executor,* proving they have legal authority to act on behalf of the estate. Banks and other institutions often ask to see this before releasing funds or information to an executor.

Fiduciary. Anyone *legally required to act in someone else's best interest instead of their own.* An executor, a power of attorney, and a trustee are all examples of a fiduciary. If you hire a financial advisor, ask directly whether they act as a fiduciary, since **not all of them are required to**.

Trust. A legal arrangement where *property is held and managed by one person or institution, called a trustee,* for the benefit of another person. Some married couples set up a trust together while both are alive specifically so that property *passes to the survivor without probate at all.* If you are not sure whether your spouse set one up, look through their paperwork for anything labeled a trust, or ask the attorney who handled your spouse's estate planning if there was one.

Codicil. A written amendment to an existing will, used to make a small change without rewriting the whole document. If your spouse's will has one or more codicils attached, all of them are read together as part of the will.

Payable on death, or POD, and transfer on death, or TOD. A designation added to a bank account or investment account that names *who the money goes to when the account holder dies,* without going through probate. This works much like a beneficiary on a life insurance policy. **Chapter 9** explains how this affects accounts that were only in your spouse's name.

Small estate affidavit. A simplified legal form, allowed in most states for estates below a certain value, that *lets property transfer to heirs without a full probate court process.* **Chapter 8** explains when this option might apply to you.

Words that sound similar but mean different things

A few pairs of terms are easy to mix up. *A will and a trust* both control where property goes, but *a will works through probate while a trust generally does not.* A *power of attorney and a health care proxy* both let someone act for you, but *one covers money and property while the other covers medical decisions,* and they are often separate documents even though people sometimes assume one covers both. *An executor and a trustee* sound similar, and both manage someone else's property, but *an executor handles an estate through probate, while a trustee manages property held in a trust,* often without court involvement at all. If a form or a conversation ever leaves you unsure which of a pair is being discussed, it is always fair to ***stop and ask which one specifically applies to your situation.***

Keep this chapter close by

You do not need to memorize any of this. The point of reading it now is simply so that *none of these words catch you off guard later,* when you are already tired and trying to focus on a phone call or a form.

Come back to this chapter, or to the full glossary in the back of the book, any time a word trips you up. Nobody expects you to already know this vocabulary, and *asking a bank teller, a funeral director, or a government worker to explain a term in plain language is a completely reasonable thing to do every single time you need to.*

Why funeral homes and banks use these words

These words exist because they describe specific legal situations, and using the precise term avoids confusion in contracts and court filings. That is a reasonable purpose. The problem is that almost nobody explains these words to the person sitting across the desk, grieving, who is expected to just know what they mean. You are allowed to stop anyone, at any bank, funeral home, or government office, and ask them to explain a word in plain language. **This is not a foolish question**. It is a reasonable one, and a good professional will answer it without making you feel small for asking.

A running list of every term used in this book, gathered in one place, is in the **Glossary** in the back of the book, so you can flip back to it any time a word slips your mind.

Chapter 3: The First Week

This chapter walks through the practical decisions of the first week: getting death certificates, deciding on burial or cremation, and telling the people closest to you, without wearing yourself out in the process.

Getting the death certificate

A death certificate is the official record of your spouse's death. *You will need certified copies*, meaning copies with a *raised seal or stamp* from the state, **not photocopies**, for nearly every task ahead of you: closing bank accounts, filing insurance claims, transferring a car title, and applying for survivor benefits.

The funeral home you choose will almost always handle the paperwork to request certified copies on your behalf as part of their standard service. *This is one of the most helpful things a funeral home does,* and it means you usually do not have to visit a government office yourself.

How many copies do you need? Most people need somewhere *between eight and twelve.* Nearly every bank, insurance company, and government office wants its own certified copy, and many of them keep the copy instead of returning it to you. It is *cheaper to order extra copies up front* than to reorder one at a time later, since the price per copy usually drops after the first one.

Certified copies typically cost somewhere *between ten and thirty dollars each,* depending on your state, so ordering ten copies usually costs somewhere between $100 and $300 total. This cost is often included in, or added to, the funeral home's bill. *Ask them directly what the death certificate fee covers and how many copies are included.*

If you run out of copies later, you can always order more from your state's vital records office. The funeral home can tell you how to do this, or the resource directory in the back of this book lists where to start.

Funeral, burial, and cremation decisions

This is one of the heaviest decisions of the first week and also one where you have more time than it feels like you do. Nothing requires you to decide within hours. Most funeral homes will hold your spouse's body for several days while you make arrangements, and cremation providers typically allow even more time.

There are two basic paths: *burial or cremation.* Within each path, there is a wide range of what you spend, and the difference is almost entirely in what services and products you choose to add.

Burial. A funeral with a viewing and burial, including a casket, the funeral home's services, and basic costs, runs on average *close to $9,000 in 2026* and *closer to $11,000 when a burial vault is included, which many cemeteries require.* This total usually does not include the cemetery plot itself or a headstone, which are billed separately by the cemetery and can add several thousand dollars more. When you add the plot, a headstone, flowers, an obituary, and a gathering afterward, a full burial commonly lands somewhere between $11,000 and $13,000.

Cremation. A funeral with a viewing followed by cremation runs on average close to $7,000, mostly because it still includes the same viewing and service costs as a burial. *A direct cremation, meaning no viewing or funeral service, just the cremation itself, is far less expensive.* Direct cremation typically costs somewhere between $1,500 and $3,500, depending on your location and the provider.

Cremation societies and prepaid plans. Companies like the Neptune Society specialize in direct cremation and often cost less than a traditional funeral home for the same basic service. Neptune Society's direct cremation packages typically run between $1,600 and $2,500, and they also sell prepaid membership plans, often starting around $2,000, with payment plans available for a set amount per month. A prepaid plan can lock in today's price against future increases, which is worth knowing if your spouse had already arranged one or if you are now thinking ahead to your own arrangements.

If your spouse already had a prepaid funeral or cremation plan in place, look for paperwork in a file cabinet, safe, or with an attorney, and *call the company listed as soon as you can*. A prepaid plan can save you from paying for services twice.

Whichever path or provider you choose, **ask for a written, itemized price list before agreeing to anything**. Federal law requires funeral homes to give you this list, called a General Price List, if you ask for it, and it lets you see exactly what you are paying for instead of one lump sum. It is reasonable and common to call more than one funeral home or cremation provider and compare their price lists before deciding. A grieving family calling around for prices is not being disrespectful. It is being careful with money that matters.

Veterans. If your spouse served in the military, ask the funeral home about veterans' burial benefits right away, since these can lower your out-of-pocket cost. As of 2026, the Department of Veterans Affairs pays a burial allowance of up to $1,000 for a death not related to service and up to $2,000 if the death was related to a service-connected condition. The VA can also provide a burial plot in a national cemetery at no cost, along with a headstone or marker. Be careful of anyone contacting you first and promising a much larger payment than this in exchange for personal information. That is a scam, not a benefit, and it is covered further in **Chapter 10.**

Comparing a traditional funeral home to a cremation society. A full-service funeral home handles everything: the viewing, the service, transportation, and either burial or cremation. A cremation society, like the Neptune Society or similar regional companies, specializes specifically in direct cremation and strips away the parts of a traditional funeral you may not want or need, which is why their prices run lower. Neither type of provider is automatically better than the other. A traditional funeral home makes sense if you want a viewing, a religious service, or a burial.

A cremation society makes sense if a simple, direct cremation with no viewing is what your spouse wanted or what your budget calls for. Some families choose a hybrid: a small gathering or memorial service held later, separate from the cremation itself, which can cost far less than a funeral home service held around the body.

What Neptune Society specifically offers. Neptune Society is a national cremation provider with local offices in many states. Their core service is direct cremation, meaning your spouse's body is cremated without an accompanying funeral service, and the cremated remains are returned to you. Beyond the direct cremation itself, they offer optional add-ons such as *an urn, a memorial service, and shipping of remains,* each priced separately, which is a *common source of confusion.* Ask for every cost in writing, itemized, before signing anything, so a quoted price of around $2,000 does not quietly grow once add-ons are included. Note that Neptune Society, like many providers, has periodically raised its prices, so treat any price mentioned in this book, or anywhere else, as *an estimate to confirm directly with them, not a guarantee.*

Comparing prices between providers. It is worth calling at least two or three funeral homes or cremation providers, whether that includes Neptune Society, a similar national cremation company, or a locally owned funeral home, and comparing their written price lists side by side. Prices for the same basic direct cremation can vary by hundreds of dollars between providers in the same area, with no difference in the quality of care your spouse receives. A locally owned funeral home is sometimes less expensive than a national company and sometimes more, so this only becomes clear by actually calling around and asking.

Green or natural burial. Some cemeteries offer green burial, sometimes called natural burial, which skips embalming, a metal casket, and a concrete vault, *using a biodegradable casket or shroud instead.* This is usually less expensive than a conventional burial and is chosen by some families for environmental or personal reasons. Not every cemetery offers this option, so ask directly whether a green burial section exists locally if this interests you.

Home funerals. In most states, it is legal for a family to care for their own deceased loved one at home, without a funeral home handling the body, at least for part of the process. This is uncommon and requires specific state paperwork, so if this interests you, search for a home funeral guide or a home funeral network specific to your state before deciding, since the legal requirements vary significantly.

Religious and cultural considerations. If your faith or culture has specific requirements or traditions around death, such as a specific timeline for burial, a particular way the body must be prepared, or restrictions around cremation, tell the funeral home this directly and early. Most funeral homes are experienced working with a range of religious and cultural practices and can adjust their standard process to fit yours. If your place of worship has clergy who regularly assist with these arrangements, involve them as early as you are able to.

What to do if you cannot afford a funeral. If cost is a serious barrier, ask the funeral home directly about their lowest-cost options before assuming you cannot afford anything beyond what was first quoted. Many counties also offer indigent burial or cremation assistance for residents who cannot afford services, administered through the county or state, and a funeral home or hospital social worker can often point you toward this program by name. Some nonprofit and religious organizations also offer emergency funeral assistance. None of this is a sign of failure. Funerals are expensive by design, and needing help paying for one is common, not shameful.

Organ and body donation. If your spouse had registered as an organ donor, this process is typically handled immediately by the hospital or organ procurement organization at the time of death, before a funeral home is even involved, and it does not prevent a funeral or viewing afterward in most cases. Whole-body donation to a medical school or research program is a separate and less common choice, usually arranged in advance, that can reduce or eliminate funeral costs entirely, since the receiving institution typically covers transportation and cremation, later returning the cremated remains to the family. If your spouse expressed interest in this and you are not sure whether arrangements were made, a local medical school's body donation program can tell you quickly whether they are registered.

No right answer. *There is no correct choice between burial and cremation,* and no single provider that is right for every family. What matters is choosing something you can afford and can live with, not something you feel pressured into because a funeral home suggested it or because it is what other people in your family expected. If your spouse left written wishes, follow them if you are able to. If they did not, you are allowed to choose based on what makes sense for you.

Notifying close family and friends without wearing yourself out

You do not have to make every phone call yourself. Ask one trusted person, a sibling, a close friend, or a member of your church or community to help spread the word to the wider circle of people who should know. You make the first few calls to the people closest to you, the ones who need to hear it from you directly, and let someone else carry the rest of the message outward.

A short, simple message works fine for people further out: "*I'm sorry to share that [name] passed away on [date]. Services will be [date/details], or I'll share those soon.*" You do not owe anyone details you are not ready to give.

Accepting help from neighbors and friends in this window

This is the week to *say yes to help*, even if saying yes does not come naturally to you. If a neighbor offers to bring a meal, say yes. If a friend offers to sit with you while you make calls, say yes. If someone offers a ride to the funeral home, say yes. You are not a burden. People who offer to help in this first week generally mean it, and letting them help gives them a way to show up for you that they need almost as much as you need the help itself.

If you live with a disability and normally relied on your spouse for physical tasks, transportation, or daily routines, this first week is the moment to be specific about what you need instead of hoping someone guesses. "*Can you drive me to the funeral home Thursday at ten?*" is easier for a friend to say yes to than a vague offer left open-ended. **Chapter 16** goes into building this kind of support further out, but for this first week, keep it simple: ask for exactly what you need, one request at a time.

One man's story

A man we will call Walter, who used a wheelchair and had lost his wife after forty years of marriage, found himself unable to get to the funeral home the first day because his usual ride, his wife, was gone. He sat with the phone for an hour before he called his next-door neighbor, someone he had waved to for years but never really asked for anything. The neighbor came within twenty minutes. Over that first week, Walter learned to ask directly instead of hinting: "A ride here." "A hand carrying boxes there," and "Someone to sit with him during the viewing so he was not alone." He said later that the hardest part was not asking himself, once he tried it, but believing beforehand that people would actually say, "Yes." They did.

PART 2: The First 30 Days

This part moves from the funeral into the paperwork that comes with a deadline. None of it requires you to travel or stand in a long line if that is hard for you right now. *Most of it can be done by mail, by phone, or online*. You will build a simple system for tracking everything, work through reporting the death to Social Security and other agencies, notify the everyday accounts and institutions that need to know, and, if you live with a disability yourself, learn the extra steps that protect the benefits you already rely on. None of this needs to happen in a single sitting, and the pace you set is entirely up to you.

Chapter 4: Getting the Paperwork Started

The first thirty days are *mostly about paperwork,* and paperwork goes easier when you have a system before you start, instead of a growing pile on the kitchen table. This is the time when you have to sort things out and create categories so that it's easier for you in the long run.

How many certified copies do you actually need, and who wants an original?

Chapter 3 covered ordering certified copies of the death certificate. Here is how they actually get used. Some places, like the Social Security Administration, *only need to see a copy* and will hand it back or accept a photocopy. Other places, like most banks, insurance companies, and the county recorder's office for a house deed, *want to keep an original certified copy permanently*. Before you mail or hand over a certified copy, ask whether it will be returned. If the answer is no, you are spending one of your copies, and you should track that.

Building a simple system to track everything

You do not need anything fancy. A cardboard box, a folder, or an accordion file works. What matters is having one place where every piece of paper goes, instead of several piles in several rooms.

A simple system that works for most people:

1. One folder or section for death certificates and **funeral paperwork.**
2. One folder or section for anything related to **Social Security and other government benefits**.
3. One folder or section for **bank, credit card, and financial account** paperwork.
4. One folder or section for **insurance,** including life insurance and health insurance.
5. One folder or section for anything related to the **house, car, or other property.**
6. *One folder or section for anything you are not sure where to put yet. It is fine to have a "sort later" pile.*

Keep a blank tracking sheet somewhere, perhaps on the fridge. Provide yourself with columns for the date you contacted each place, who you spoke with, what they asked for, and what happened next. Filling this in as you go, even briefly, saves you from having to remember details weeks later when someone calls back asking a follow-up question. You might want to make a spreadsheet of this on your computer so that it is easier to print it out whenever you wish to have a copy. Spreadsheet templates are included in all document programs such as Word for PC or Mac.

Doing this by mail or phone when leaving the house is hard

Nearly everything in this chapter and the next few chapters *can be done without leaving your home.* Social Security can be reached by phone. Most banks and insurance companies have paperwork you can mail in, along with a phone number for questions. If a task seems to require an in-person visit, *call first and ask directly whether it can be done by mail or phone instead.* Many offices have options for people who cannot travel; **they do not advertise unless you ask.**

If you must visit somewhere in person and getting there is difficult, ask a friend, a neighbor, or a local volunteer service to drive you, or ask whether the office offers *a home visit or a video call option.* Area Agencies on Aging, covered fully in **Chapter 16**, often know about local transportation help for exactly this kind of appointment.

Pacing yourself through the list

Thirty days sounds short, but *almost nothing in this book has a true thirty-day deadline.* Most institutions understand that a death in the family takes time to sort out, and a short delay rarely causes a real problem. Work through your tracking sheet a few items at a time rather than trying to finish it all in one sitting. A single productive phone call a day, some days, is a completely reasonable pace.

If a piece of paperwork gets lost

Paperwork gets lost sometimes, whether in the mail, in an office, or in your own house during a hard week. If a company says they never received something you mailed, ask if they can accept it by fax, secure upload, or email attachment instead, which is often faster to confirm than mail. *Keep a copy of everything you send, whether a photocopy or a photograph taken with your phone, so you are never left with no proof that something was sent.* Always consider whether it would be prudent to *send anything via certified mail* so that someone will have to sign for it when it gets to the receiving party.

Handling calls that come at inconvenient times

Institutions do not always call back at a convenient moment, and it is easy to feel like you must answer every time or lose your place in line. In reality, most companies will call again, or you can call the direct number they gave you and reference your case or claim number. Keeping that number written down, alongside the date and the name of whoever you last spoke with, saves you from starting an explanation over from the beginning every time you call.

A note on time zones and business hours

Government offices, including Social Security, generally operate on business hours in their local time zone, and hold times are often shortest right when they open in the morning. If you have tried calling in the afternoon with long waits, try again first thing in the morning instead, and keep something to occupy your hands or mind nearby, since some calls take a while even at the best times.

If the workload feels like too much for one person

If you are managing this process while also managing a disability, a full-time job, or caregiving for someone else, it is reasonable to *ask a trusted friend or family member to help you work through the tracking sheet,* make some of the phone calls, or simply sit with you while you make them. Some professional organizers and daily money managers, listed in the resource directory, specialize in helping people through exactly this kind of process for a fee, which may be worth it if no one close to you is available to help.

Chapter 5: Money That Stops and Money That Starts

This chapter is about the money side of the first thirty days: **what income stops, what benefits start,** and how to file the claims that get money moving in your direction again.

Reporting the death to Social Security

Call the Social Security Administration at 1-800-772-1213 **as soon as you can**. Social Security cannot be notified by email or through their website. You must call or visit an office in person, and calling is almost always easier. If your spouse was receiving benefits, the funeral home may also report the death to Social Security for you as part of their standard paperwork, but *it is worth confirming this happened rather than assuming it did.*

There is a one-time payment of $250 available to a surviving spouse in most cases. Ask about this directly when you call, since it is easy for it to get lost in a longer conversation about ongoing benefits.

Applying for survivor benefits

If you are sixty or older, you likely qualify for Social Security survivor benefits based on your spouse's work record, as long as you were married at least nine months. If you are between fifty and fifty-nine and have a disability that began within seven years of your spouse's death, you may also qualify. If you are caring for your spouse's child who is under sixteen or who has a disability, you may qualify at any age. Often, a social worker at a community agency can help you with the exact Social Security rules that relate to your individual benefits or needs.

If you are under sixty and do not fall into one of these categories yet, it is still worth calling to ask about your specific timeline, since the rules include enough exceptions that *it is easy to assume you do not qualify when you actually do, or will soon*. Mark your calendar for when you might become eligible if that applies to you, since Social Security generally does not pay retroactive benefits for months you were eligible but did not apply.

Survivor benefits typically run between about seventy-one and one hundred percent of what your spouse's benefit was, depending on your age when you start receiving them. If you were already receiving a spousal benefit based on your spouse's record while they were alive, Social Security usually switches you to the survivor benefit automatically once the death is reported, but it is still worth calling to confirm this happened correctly.

You cannot apply for survivor benefits online. You must call 1-800-772-1213, Monday through Friday, or visit a local Social Security office. Be ready for hold times. Calling early in the morning, right when lines open, often means a shorter wait.

Pensions, annuities, and retirement accounts

If your spouse had a pension through an employer or a union, contact the pension office directly. Ask specifically *whether the pension included a survivor benefit,* meaning a portion of the pension that continues to be paid to you. Not all pensions include this, and some require the surviving spouse to have been named at the time the pension started, so this is an important question to ask early.

For annuities and retirement accounts like a 401(k) or an IRA, contact the company that manages the account. If you were named as the beneficiary, which is common for a spouse, the funds usually transfer to you directly *without going through probate.* You will need a certified death certificate and a claim form from the company.

Filing a life insurance claim

If your spouse had a life insurance policy, whether through an employer or purchased separately, look for the policy paperwork, or check with the employer's human resources office if it was a workplace policy. Once you find the insurance company, *call their claims department.* They will send you a claim form, and you will need to submit it along with a *certified copy of the death certificate.* Insurers typically pay out within a few days to a few weeks once they have everything they need, so submitting a complete claim the first time, rather than piece by piece, speeds things up considerably.

If you are not sure whether your spouse had a life insurance policy at all, check old mail, tax returns for any mention of premiums paid, and any employer paperwork. Some states also have an unclaimed property search you can use, listed in the resource directory, in case a policy exists that no one has claimed yet.

Are survivor benefits and life insurance payouts taxed

Life insurance proceeds paid to you as a beneficiary are generally not counted as taxable income at the federal level. Social Security survivor benefits *may be partly taxable* depending on your total income, similar to how regular Social Security benefits are treated. This is a good question to *bring to a tax preparer* when you file your next tax return, especially the first year, since your filing status and household income will have changed. **Chapter 12** covers rebuilding your budget, and **Chapter 15** covers finding low-cost tax help.

If you were married more than once

If you were previously divorced and remarried, this generally does not complicate your survivor benefit as the current spouse. However, if your current spouse was previously married and divorced, and that former spouse never remarried, it is worth knowing that *a former spouse may also be eligible for survivor benefits* based on the same work record, separately from yours. Benefits paid to a former spouse do not reduce what you receive. This sometimes comes as a surprise to families and is worth understanding rather than being blindsided by later.

What happens to a joint bank account

If your bank account was jointly owned with your spouse, the account typically becomes yours alone automatically, and you generally keep access to it. Still, call the bank to let them know of the death and ask what, if anything, they need from you, such as a certified death certificate for their records. If the account was only in your spouse's name, it may be frozen once the bank learns of the death, and accessing those funds may require going through the executor and, in some cases, probate. **Chapter 8** explains this process.

One Social Security story

A widow we will call Delores reported her husband's death to Social Security *the same week he died*, mostly because a friend told her not to wait. Her survivor benefit began within about six weeks. A neighbor of hers, a widower we will call Frank, *put off the call for nearly two months* because the idea of explaining it out loud on the phone felt unbearable. When he finally called, everything worked out, but he had gone two extra months on a smaller income than he needed to, and he had to catch up on bills in the meantime. *Neither of them did anything wrong.* Grief slows people down in ways that make complete sense. *But this is one call where making it sooner,* even before you feel ready, genuinely helps your bank account later.

Chapter 6: Telling the Right People, in the Right Order

Beyond the government and the insurance companies, there is a longer list of everyday accounts and relationships that need to know your spouse has died. This chapter gives you an order to work through it in, so you are not trying to remember everything at once.

Banks, credit cards, and the mortgage or landlord

Call your bank first, as covered in **Chapter 5**. Then call any credit card company where your spouse was the primary account holder or a joint holder. If a card was only in your spouse's name, it typically needs to be closed rather than transferred, and *any balance becomes part of the estate* rather than your personal responsibility, in most states.

If you have a mortgage, call the mortgage company to let them know of the death, especially if your spouse was the only name on the loan. Federal law protects you from being forced off the home or having the loan called due just because of the death, and most mortgage companies will work with you to keep the loan in your name going forward. If you rent, notify your landlord, both out of common courtesy and because your lease may have your spouse's name on it, *which could affect renewal.*

Utilities, phone, and subscriptions in a joint name

Work through utility bills, one at a time: electric, gas, water, phone, and internet. Most companies will simply update the name on the account with a copy of the death certificate. Subscriptions, whether streaming services, memberships, or smaller recurring charges, can wait, but it is worth going through a recent bank or credit card statement at some point in the first month to *catch anything billing automatically* that you no longer need.

The employer, and any union or pension office

If your spouse was still working at the time of death, contact the employer's human resources department. Ask about any final paycheck owed, unused vacation pay, life insurance through the job, and whether the pension or retirement plan requires separate notification, since sometimes HR and the plan administrator are different offices. If your spouse belonged to a union, contact the union office directly as well, since unions sometimes provide a death benefit separate from anything through the employer.

If your spouse was self-employed

If your spouse ran their own business or worked as an independent contractor, there is no human resources office to call, which means a few extra steps fall to you. Look for a business partner, an accountant, or a bookkeeper your spouse worked with, since they can help you understand outstanding invoices, business debts, and clients who need to be notified. If the business had its own bank accounts, insurance policies, or a business entity like an LLC, these may need separate attention from your personal accounts, and an accountant or attorney familiar with small businesses can help you sort out what needs to happen with the business itself, including whether to continue, sell, or close it.

Government and licensing offices

A few less obvious places may also need to know: the Department of Motor Vehicles, to cancel or transfer a driver's license record, and any professional licensing board if your spouse held a professional license, such as for a trade, medicine, law, or another regulated profession. These are rarely urgent, but working through them eventually helps prevent confusion, such as *unexpected renewal notices or licensing fees* arriving in the following year.

Keeping the list from feeling endless

It can start to feel like this list has no end, especially in weeks when you find one more account or one more company that needs a call. That feeling is common, and it does ease. Most people find that the bulk of these calls cluster in the first month or two, with only occasional loose ends afterward. Crossing items off your tracking sheet, even slowly, is real progress, even on the days it does not feel that way.

A one-page checklist, in order

1. Bank accounts
2. Credit cards
3. Mortgage or landlord
4. Utilities: electric, gas, water
5. Phone and internet
6. Employer, if still working
7. Union or pension office, if applicable
8. Subscriptions and memberships, when you have time

This same list appears again in the First 30 Days Checklist in the back of the book, check off as you go.

Accounts you might not think of right away

Beyond the obvious accounts, a few others are easy to overlook. *Frequent flyer miles and hotel loyalty points* sometimes can be transferred to a surviving spouse; contact the program directly and ask about their policy, since it varies by company. Streaming services, cloud photo storage, and email accounts often hold photos and messages that matter to you, so before canceling anything, *consider downloading or saving what you want to keep.* If your spouse kept a list of passwords, either written down or in a password manager, this is the moment that list becomes valuable. If no such list exists, many services have a process for a surviving spouse to request access or a memorialized account, though it typically requires a death certificate and can take time.

If a bill shows up later that you did not expect

It is common for a bill or statement to arrive weeks or months after a death for an account you had not gotten to yet or did not know existed. This is not a sign you did something wrong. Simply add it to your tracking sheet and work through it the same way as everything else: a phone call, a certified death certificate if requested, and a note of what was resolved.

Chapter 7: If You Live With a Disability, a Few Extra Steps

If you receive disability benefits yourself, either SSDI or SSI, there are *a few extra things worth understanding right away,* because getting them wrong can accidentally reduce or pause a benefit you depend on. At this point, if you haven't already contacted someone, it might be helpful to speak to a social worker who knows how to navigate this particular situation.

How survivor benefits can affect SSDI or SSI

SSDI, Social Security Disability Insurance, and SSI, Supplemental Security Income, work differently, and this matters a great deal here. SSDI is based on your own work record or your spouse's work record, and it can generally be received alongside a survivor benefit, sometimes combined into one adjusted payment. SSI is *based on financial need, not work history,* and receiving a new survivor benefit or a lump sum, such as life insurance proceeds, can affect how much SSI you receive, because SSI has strict limits on income and resources.

Do not assume how this will work in your specific case. Call Social Security directly and ask them to explain how a survivor benefit, or any lump sum you receive, will affect your SSI specifically, before you accept or spend any of it. This one phone call *can prevent a benefit reduction* that is much harder to fix after the fact.

Protecting benefits you already receive while new paperwork is in motion

While you are reporting the death and filing new claims, keep close track of any deadlines. Social Security or another agency gives you a form for reporting changes in income or resources. If you receive a lump sum from life insurance or a pension, ask specifically how quickly it needs to be reported and whether spending it in a certain way, such as on funeral costs already paid, is treated differently. These rules are detailed and specific to your situation, which is exactly why *asking directly, rather than guessing, protects you.*

Updating your own power of attorney and health care proxy

If your spouse was named as your power of attorney or your health care proxy, meaning the person authorized to make decisions for you if you become unable to, that authority ended when they died. This is worth addressing soon, not because anything is wrong right now, but because an emergency does not wait for convenient timing. **Chapter 11** walks through how to name someone new.

Requesting accommodations from agencies and offices, in writing

If a disability makes phone hold times, paperwork, or travel especially difficult, you are allowed to *ask agencies for accommodations,* such as a callback instead of a hold, a written summary of a phone conversation, or extra time to submit documents. *Making this request in writing,* even a short email or letter, creates a record of what was asked and agreed to, which can help if there is ever a dispute later about a missed deadline.

A woman we will call Nadia, who received SSI due to a chronic illness, received a life insurance payout a few weeks after her husband died and *did not think to report it right away,* since she was still deep in funeral bills and grief. A caseworker later flagged the deposit, and her SSI was reduced for a period while the agency sorted out the timeline. Once she explained what had happened and provided records showing the money had gone toward funeral and medical costs, her benefit was corrected and back payments were issued. It took a few stressful months to resolve. Nadia said afterward that she wished someone had told her, in the first week, to call and ask before spending or reporting anything, instead of finding out the rule after she had already broken it by accident.

If you have a representative payee

If someone else, perhaps your spouse, was serving as your representative payee, meaning the person Social Security designated to manage your benefit payments on your behalf, this role ends when they die and a new payee needs to be established if you still need one. Call Social Security to discuss this directly. If you are able to manage your own benefits now, you can also ask about becoming your own payee going forward.

Medicare and prescription costs after a change in income

If your income drops after your spouse's death, you may newly qualify for programs that help with Medicare costs, such as a Medicare Savings Program, which can help pay premiums and other costs, or Extra Help, which lowers the cost of prescription drug coverage. These programs are easy to miss because they are not automatic. Ask about both specifically when you get your free benefits check-up, covered in **Chapter 13**.

Returning to work later, if that becomes relevant

If you receive SSDI and think you might want to try returning to work at some point, ask Social Security about the *Ticket to Work program*, which allows a trial work period without immediately losing your benefit. This is not urgent to sort out now, but it is worth knowing this option exists for whenever, or if, it becomes relevant to you.

Keeping a written record of every disability-related call

Because benefit rules affecting disability are especially detailed, *keep a written record* specifically for these calls: *the date, who you spoke with, what they told you, and any reference or confirmation number* given. Again, *another spreadsheet might be helpful here.* If a benefit is ever incorrectly reduced or paused, as happened to Nadia in the story above, this record becomes your strongest evidence for getting it corrected quickly, since agencies often move faster once you can point to exactly what was said and when.

You are allowed to ask the same question twice

If an answer from an agency does not sound right or contradicts something you read here or heard elsewhere, you are allowed to call back and ask again, ideally speaking with someone else the second time. Phone representatives are human and occasionally give incomplete or incorrect information, particularly on complicated interactions between programs like SSDI, SSI, and survivor benefits. A second call that confirms or corrects the first one is a reasonable use of your time, not a nuisance.

PART 3: Legal Matters

This part explains *probate, property, and legal protection* in plain terms, with attention to how things work differently *when there are no children*. You will learn what a will actually controls and what happens without one, how a house, car, and other property transfer into your name, how to recognize and protect yourself from the scams that specifically target grieving spouses, and how to update your own legal documents now that your spouse can no longer serve as your power of attorney or health care proxy. None of this requires a law degree to understand. It only requires knowing which questions to ask and who to ask them of.

Chapter 8: Wills and What Happens Without One

Probate is the court process that settles a person's estate after death. A judge confirms the will is valid, if there is one, and officially puts the executor in charge of paying debts and distributing what is left. Probate exists to make sure everything is handled fairly and legally, but it also takes time, sometimes months, and in *some states it can cost money in court fees.*

Not everything goes through probate. Anything with a named beneficiary, like a life insurance policy or a retirement account, or anything owned jointly with survivorship, like many houses and bank accounts, usually passes directly to the surviving person without probate. **Chapter 9** explains this further for property specifically. Probate mainly deals with what is left over: things owned only in your spouse's name, without a beneficiary listed.

Many states also have a simplified process for smaller estates, sometimes called a small estate affidavit, which skips much of the formal probate process if the total value is below a certain amount. Ask a probate court clerk or a low-cost legal aid office, listed in the resource directory, whether your situation qualifies.

What a will does and does not control

A will names who inherits property, names an executor, and can name a guardian for minor children. *A will does not control anything with its own named beneficiary, such as a life insurance policy or a retirement account.* Those pass to whoever is named on that specific account, regardless of what the will says. This is a common source of confusion, and it is worth checking that the beneficiaries listed on your spouse's accounts actually matched what they intended, since an outdated beneficiary form overrides a will every time.

Why having no children changes who inherits what

If your spouse had a valid will, it names who inherits, and having no children does not change that. The confusion comes in when there is no will. Every state has its own set of rules, called *intestate succession*, that decide who inherits when there is no will. In most states, if you have no children, the surviving spouse inherits everything, or nearly everything. But in some states, *if your spouse had living parents or siblings, those relatives may be entitled to a share of the estate alongside you*, even though you were married and there are no children. This surprises a lot of people.

Because these rules vary significantly by state, this is a case where a short conversation with a probate court clerk or a *low-cost legal aid attorney* is worth having early, rather than assuming you know the answer. It costs little to ask and can prevent a serious misunderstanding with in-laws later.

What an executor actually does, step by step

If you are named executor, or if the court appoints you because there was no will, the job generally involves these steps, roughly in order:

- filing the will with the probate court, if there is one
- obtaining a letter testamentary, the document proving your legal authority
- identifying and gathering the estate's assets
- notifying known creditors and paying valid debts from estate funds
- filing a final tax return for your spouse
- distributing what remains to the rightful heirs

A probate court clerk can explain your specific state's filing requirements, and *many courts have self-help forms or a self-help center for* ***estates that do not require an attorney,*** particularly smaller or simpler ones.

How long probate typically takes

Probate timelines vary a great deal by state and by how complicated the estate is, but a simple, uncontested estate often takes somewhere *between six months and a year to fully close*, while a more complicated one can take longer. This is not a sign anything has gone wrong. It reflects required waiting periods for creditors to come forward, court schedules, and the time it takes to properly account for everything. Many of the practical steps in this book, like accessing a jointly held bank account or receiving a beneficiary payout, do not wait for probate to finish, which is part of why it is worth understanding what does and does not depend on the probate process completing.

If you are not named executor

If someone else, a sibling of your spouse's, for example, is named executor instead of you, *you are still entitled to information about the estate as an heir,* and you can ask the executor directly for updates. If you believe the executor is not handling the estate properly, a probate court clerk or an attorney can explain what options exist to raise a concern with the court.

If in-laws or extended family raise questions about inheritance

Even where the law is clearly on your side, grief sometimes brings out tension in a family, particularly around money and belongings. If your spouse's parents or siblings raise questions about what they believe they are owed, it is fine to respond calmly that you are following the legal process and that a probate court clerk or attorney can confirm the details for anyone who wants to ask. *You do not need to justify your inheritance or negotiate informally out of guilt or a desire to keep the peace.* If tension escalates into a genuine legal dispute, this is exactly the kind of situation where *consulting a probate attorney directly*, rather than trying to resolve it yourself, protects both the relationship and your legal position.

Chapter 9: Property, Titles, and Deeds

The house: how the deed transfers

How your house transfers to you depends entirely on how it was titled, meaning *whose name is on the deed* and how. If the deed lists you and your spouse as "*joint tenants with right of survivorship*," or in some states as holding the property as "tenants by the entirety," the house becomes fully yours automatically the moment your spouse dies. You typically just need to file a certified copy of the death certificate with the county recorder's office to update the record, which the funeral home or a title company can often help arrange.

If the deed was only in your spouse's name, or if it listed you as "tenants in common" rather than with survivorship, the house may need to go through probate before it legally transfers to you. This is worth checking directly by *requesting a copy of your deed from the county recorder's office* if you are not sure how it was titled.

The car and other titled property

Cars, boats, and other titled property work similarly to a house, though the process for transferring a title is usually handled through your state's motor vehicle office rather than a county recorder. Bring a certified death certificate, the current title, and your identification, and ask directly what their specific process requires, since it varies by state.

Retitling accounts that were only in a spouse's name

For any account that was only in your spouse's name, without you listed as a joint owner or beneficiary, contact the bank or company directly and ask what they need to either transfer or close the account. This usually requires proof that you are the executor or a small estate affidavit if your state allows one for accounts of that size, along with a certified death certificate.

Mobile homes, timeshares, and other unusual property

Mobile and manufactured homes are sometimes titled like a vehicle rather than like real estate, depending on your state, so check with your state's motor vehicle office as well as the county recorder if you are not sure which applies. Timeshares transfer according to the specific contract your spouse signed, and some timeshare companies charge a transfer fee or require you to formally accept or decline the timeshare as part of the estate, so read the original contract or call the company directly to understand your options, including the option to walk away from it if it is more burden than benefit.

If your spouse owned part of a business

If your spouse owned or co-owned a business, the way it transfers depends heavily on *how it was legally structured and whether a partnership agreement or operating agreement* addressed what happens when an owner dies. This is a situation *worth bringing to an attorney fairly early*, since ongoing business operations, employees, and contracts may need attention sooner than other parts of the estate.

If a lender resists working with you

Occasionally a mortgage company or lender is slow to update records or makes the process harder than it should be after a death. *Federal law specifically protects a surviving spouse's right to stay on a mortgage and assume the loan without requalifying in most circumstances.* If a lender is not cooperating, the Consumer Financial Protection Bureau, listed in the resource directory, accepts complaints about exactly this kind of situation and can be a useful next step.

Homeowners and auto insurance

Do not overlook updating your homeowners insurance and auto insurance policies, since both often list your spouse as a named policyholder, and a lapse in coverage or an outdated policy could cause a problem if you ever need to file a claim. Call your insurance agent, let them know of the death, and confirm the policy is updated correctly in your name alone.

Property that was truly shared informally

Sometimes a couple owns things together in practice, like a car both of you drove and a shared savings account earmarked for something specific, without formal joint ownership on paper. If it is unclear whether something was legally jointly owned or only informally shared, this is *worth asking a probate court clerk or legal aid attorney about directly,* since the answer affects whether that specific item needs to go through the estate process or not.

Personal belongings without a formal title

Furniture, jewelry, tools, and other everyday belongings usually do not have a title or deed at all, and legally they typically become part of the estate to be handled according to the will, or according to your state's intestate rules if there was no will. In practice, for most families, this part is handled informally and without conflict: the surviving spouse simply keeps the household's belongings. Disagreements are more likely if other close relatives feel entitled to specific sentimental items. If you anticipate any disagreement here, it can help to document, even with a simple photo and note, what you intend to keep and why, particularly for anything of real financial or sentimental value.

Storage units and property in a spouse's name only

If your spouse rented a storage unit, a safe deposit box, or held other property in their name alone that you did not have access to, contact the company or bank directly and ask what is required for you, as spouse or executor, to gain access. A certified death certificate and proof of your role in the estate are typically enough, though a safe deposit box sometimes requires additional steps depending on your state and the bank's own policy.

Chapter 10: Protecting Yourself From Scams

Grief is exhausting, and scammers know it. This chapter is about recognizing the specific scams that target grieving spouses, especially disabled and older widows and widowers, so you can protect yourself during a time when your guard may naturally be down.

Common scams that specifically target you right now

Fake benefits officials. Someone calls or shows up claiming to represent Social Security, the VA, or another agency, saying you are owed money but need to "verify" personal information first, like your Social Security number or bank account. *Real government agencies do not call you out of the blue demanding personal information to release a benefit.*

Obituary scammers. Some scammers read published obituaries and use the details—your spouse's name, your address, and your city—to sound convincing when they call, claiming your spouse owed a debt or left an unpaid bill. This is why some people choose not to include a home address in a published obituary. One hint here: if someone is presenting themselves from a corporation or a government agency, *look carefully at the email address they have used* if you received this type of email. Scammers generally use gmail.com, while corporations and governments do not.

Fake debt collectors. Someone calls claiming your spouse owed money and pressures you to pay immediately. *You are not personally responsible for your spouse's individual debts in most cases*, only debts you co-signed or joint debts. *Ask for everything in writing* before paying anything, and verify independently rather than trusting a caller's word.

Unsolicited financial advisors or insurance sellers. Someone learns of the death, often through an obituary or public records, and reaches out offering to "help" you manage a life insurance payout or invest your survivor benefit. A reputable financial professional does not cold-call a grieving widow within days of a death.

Warning signs

Pressure to decide or pay immediately. Requests for personal information over the phone or by email from someone who contacted you first. Promises of a much larger government benefit than what the actual program pays, as covered in **Chapter 3** regarding VA burial benefits. Anyone asking you to *pay by gift card, wire transfer, or cryp-*

tocurrency, which are all signs of a scam regardless of the story attached to them.

What to do if you think you've already been targeted

Contact the AARP Fraud Watch Network Helpline at 877-908-3360. This free service offers guidance whether or not you are an AARP member. You can also report fraud to the Federal Trade Commission at reportfraud.ftc.gov, and if the scam involved a claim of VA benefits specifically, report it to the VA's fraud hotline at 833-388-7233. If money has already been sent, *contact your bank immediately*, since some transfers can still be stopped or reversed if caught quickly.

One woman's scam story

A widow we will call Bernice received a phone call four days after her husband's obituary ran in the local paper. The caller said he was from a benefits office and that she was owed a large payment but needed to confirm her bank account number first to process it. Something about the urgency in his voice did not sit right with her, and she told him she would call the agency back herself using the number from an official piece of mail she had received years earlier. When she called that real number, *no such payment or department existed.* She reported the call to the AARP Fraud Watch Network the same day. Bernice said the instinct that saved her was simple: a real agency had never once called her first.

A few more patterns worth knowing

Romance scams. Some scammers specifically search obituaries and dating sites looking for newly widowed people, building a relationship over weeks or months before eventually asking for money, often citing an emergency. This can happen online or, less often, in person. Be cautious of any new relationship, in any form, that moves quickly toward *requests for money, gift cards, or financial information*, no matter how genuine the connection feels.

Home repair scams. Someone shows up unsolicited, offering to fix a roof, driveway, or another home repair, sometimes claiming to have *noticed damage during a recent storm*. They ask for *payment up front* and either do poor work or none at all. Get at least one other quote and *check a contractor's license* before paying anyone who approached you first, especially for a repair you had not already been planning.

Fake charity solicitations. Some scammers *create fake charities using your late spouse's name* shortly after an obituary runs, asking for donations "in memory of" your spouse. If you did not set up a memorial fund yourself, be skeptical of any charity contacting you directly about one, and verify independently before giving.

Setting up simple protections against future scams

A few habits reduce your risk going forward:

- Do not answer calls from unknown numbers; let them go to voicemail and call back if it seems legitimate.

- Never give personal or financial information to someone who contacted you first.

- *Consider placing a free credit freeze with the three major credit bureaus*, which prevents new accounts from being opened in your name without your explicit action to lift it. **Here is where you can do that:** Equifax Phone: 1-800-685-1111, Experian Phone: 1-888-397-3742, TransUnion Phone: 1-800-916-8800

- If you are ever unsure whether a call or letter is real, hang up or set the letter aside, and call the organization back using a number you find independently, not one provided by the caller or the letter itself.

Chapter 11: Updating Your Own Legal Documents

This is a chapter about protecting your own future, not just settling your spouse's estate.

Writing or updating your own will

If you do not have a will, or if your existing will named your spouse as the main beneficiary or executor, now is the time to update it. Without a will, your own estate will be distributed according to your state's intestate succession rules when you die, which, without children, *may include relatives you would not have chosen*. A new or updated one will let you decide this yourself.

Naming a new power of attorney and health care proxy

Since your spouse can no longer serve in either role, you need to name someone new for both your financial power of attorney and your health care proxy, sometimes called a *health care power of attorney*. Choose someone you trust and who is willing and reasonably able to act quickly if needed, such as a sibling, a close friend, or in some cases a professional fiduciary if you do not have someone in your life who fits. Talk to the person directly before naming them, so they understand what you are asking of them.

Updating beneficiary forms on every account

Go through every account that has:

- a named beneficiary
- life insurance
- retirement accounts
- bank accounts with a payable-on-death designation, and update any that still list your spouse.

These are simple forms for most companies, but it is easy to forget, and an outdated beneficiary form can send money to the wrong place, or *even back through probate unnecessarily*, if it is never updated.

Finding low-cost or free legal help for this step

You do not need an expensive attorney to update a simple will, power of attorney, or health care proxy. Legal aid organizations, often funded in part through the Older Americans Act for people over sixty, provide free or low-cost help with exactly these documents. Many state and local bar associations also offer free consultation programs. The resource directory in the back of this book lists where to start looking in your area.

Writing a letter of instruction

Beyond the formal legal documents, consider writing an informal letter of instruction for whoever will eventually handle your own affairs. This is not a legal document but a practical one:

- where important papers are kept
- a list of accounts and roughly what they contain
- computer login information, or where a password list can be found
- specific wishes about your own funeral or memorial

This is one of the most useful things you can leave behind, and it is often missing even when a formal will is not. Update it every year or two, or any time something major changes.

Storing your documents somewhere they can be found

A will, power of attorney, or health care proxy only helps if someone can actually find it when it is needed. Keep original documents somewhere secure but accessible, such as a fireproof box at home or a safe deposit box, and make sure at least one trusted person, whether your new power of attorney, a close friend, or a family member, knows exactly where to find them and how to access them. A document locked away where no one knows to look is nearly as unhelpful as no document at all.

Digital assets and online accounts

Beyond paper documents, think through what should happen to your own digital accounts and information:

- email
- social media
- online banking
- digital photos or files that matter to you. Some services allow you to name a legacy contact or specify what should happen to your account after death, often buried in the account's privacy or security settings.
- password manager, which securely stores your account passwords in one place, can also be set up to allow emergency access for a trusted person you designate. This is a small task now that can prevent a great deal of frustration for whoever manages your affairs later.

Choosing your own executor and heirs

When you update your own will, take real time to think through who you want as your executor and who you want to inherit from you. Without children, this decision is entirely yours to make, whether that means a sibling, a niece or nephew, a close friend, or a charity or cause you care about. There is no default that must be followed. Talk to whoever you name as executor beforehand so they understand the responsibility and are willing to take it on when the time comes.

Reviewing your documents again down the road

Legal and financial documents are not a one-time task. Plan to review your will, power of attorney, health care proxy, and beneficiary designations every few years, or any time something significant changes: a move, a new relationship, a new account, or a change in health. A brief annual reminder, perhaps around the same time each year, is enough to keep these documents current without turning it into a constant chore.

PART 4: Building a Financial Future Alone

This part focuses on stability when there is no second income, no children to fall back on, and, for many readers, a fixed or limited income from disability. You will build a realistic monthly budget, learn how your different benefits interact and where to get a free review of all of them at once, think through your housing situation without being rushed into a decision, and find trustworthy professionals when you need help beyond what this book alone can offer. The goal throughout this part is the same: a stable, honest financial picture that you understand and control, built one clear step at a time.

Chapter 12: Making a New Budget

Listing income that stops and income that starts

Start with two simple lists. On one side, *write down every source of income that stopped when your spouse died:* a paycheck, a pension without survivor benefits, or a Social Security payment based only on their own work record. On the other side, *write down every source of income that is starting or continuing*: your own income if you work, a survivor benefit, a pension survivor benefit if one applies, and interest or withdrawals from any accounts you now control.

Listing expenses that change

Some expenses drop. A second car, certain medical costs, or a hobby that was only your spouse's. Other expenses rise, sometimes unexpectedly. A home that used to have two incomes covering it now has one. Tasks your spouse used to do, home repairs, yard work, and driving, may now cost money if you need to hire someone. Health insurance, if you were covered through your spouse's employer plan, may need to be replaced entirely, which is *often one of the biggest and most urgent expense changes to plan for.*

A simple worksheet

Make a blank budget worksheet with *three columns*:

- money coming in each month
- money going out each month
- difference between them

Fill it in with real numbers, *not guesses,* using a recent bank statement if that helps. If the number at the bottom is negative, meaning more going out than coming in, that is useful information, not a failure. It tells you clearly where to focus first, whether that is applying for a benefit you have not yet claimed, cutting an expense, or talking to a nonprofit credit counselor, covered later in this chapter.

Rebuilding an emergency fund

If your household emergency savings were depleted by funeral costs or medical bills, rebuilding even a small cushion matters, since a single unexpected expense can otherwise turn into a crisis. Start small. *Even fifty dollars set aside automatically each month,* if your budget allows it, gives you something to fall back on that did not exist before. If your budget does not allow for this yet, that is fine. *Focus first on covering essential expenses and revisit an emergency fund once your new income picture is stable.*

Dealing with debt that feels overwhelming

If bills are piling up faster than you can manage, *a nonprofit credit counseling agency,* reachable through the National Foundation for Credit Counseling, can review your full financial picture with you at little or no cost and help you build a realistic plan. This is different from a for-profit debt settlement company, which often charges high fees and can do more harm than good. *Avoid any company that contacts you directly promising to erase your debt, and instead seek out a nonprofit agency yourself.*

Your tax filing status will change

The tax year your spouse died, you can generally still file as married filing jointly, which is often the most favorable filing status. In the years after, your filing status changes, and this can affect your tax bill in ways that are easy to miss if you are simply doing what you have always done. A tax preparer, including free options through AARP Tax-Aide or the IRS Volunteer Income Tax Assistance program for those who qualify by income, both listed in the resource directory, can walk you through what changes are for your specific situation.

Revisiting your budget as things settle

Your first budget, built in the early months, is a starting point, not a permanent document. Once survivor benefits, insurance payouts, and other changes have settled into a steady pattern, usually somewhere around six months to a year after the death, it is worth revisiting the budget with more accurate numbers. Expenses and income both tend to look different once the initial disruption passes, and a second, steadier budget often looks more manageable than the first one did.

A simple monthly check-in habit

Rather than treating the budget as a one-time task, *pick a regular day each month,* perhaps when a main bill or benefit payment arrives, to glance at your accounts and confirm nothing unexpected has changed. This does not need to take more than a few minutes and can catch a billing error, a missed payment, or a benefit change early, before it becomes a bigger problem. *On your computer calendar you may be able to indicate when bills are due* or when they are paid. They can often be put in a colored font so that they stand out.

Chapter 13: Understanding Your Benefits

How benefits can overlap or affect one another

Social Security survivor benefits, SSDI, SSI, Medicare, and Medicaid interact with each other in ways that are genuinely confusing, even for people who work with them professionally. As covered in **Chapter 7**, SSDI can often be combined with a survivor benefit, while SSI has strict income and resource limits that a new survivor benefit or lump sum can affect. Medicare eligibility is generally tied to age or disability status rather than marital status, so it typically continues on its own path regardless of your spouse's death, but Medicaid eligibility is based on income and assets, which may shift once your household income changes.

Where to get a free benefits check-up

Rather than trying to work out every interaction yourself, ask for a free benefits check-up. Your local *Area Agency on Aging,* reachable through the Eldercare Locator at 1-800-677-1116, can often connect you with a benefits counselor who will review your specific situation at no cost and flag anything you might be missing or at risk of losing.

Common mistakes that cause benefits to be reduced or paused

- Not reporting a change in income or a lump sum within the required time window.
- Assuming a benefit continues automatically without confirming it.
- Spending a lump sum, like a life insurance payout, without first understanding how it affects SSI specifically, since SSI counts resources as well as income.

The safest habit is a simple one: before you make a change involving money, spend a lump sum, or assume a benefit is continuing, ***make one phone call to confirm it first.***

Other assistance programs worth checking

Beyond Social Security, Medicare, and Medicaid, a lower household income after a spouse's death sometimes newly qualifies you for other programs you were not eligible for before. *The Supplemental Nu-*

trition Assistance Program, commonly called SNAP or food stamps, helps cover grocery costs for households within certain income limits. *The Low Income Home Energy Assistance Program,* or LIHEAP, helps with heating and cooling bills. Many states also offer their own supplemental programs for older adults or people with disabilities on a fixed income. A benefits check-up through your Area Agency on Aging, mentioned above, typically screens for all of these at once, so you do not have to research each program separately.

Understanding your Medicare choices

If you are newly navigating Medicare on your own, whether because you are aging into it or because your spouse previously handled this, it helps to know the basic pieces. Original Medicare *covers hospital care and doctor visits* but leaves gaps that many people fill with a supplemental policy, sometimes called Medigap, or by choosing a Medicare Advantage plan instead, which is ***offered through a private insurer*** and often bundles in extra coverage like prescription drugs. But this may not be the choice you wish, because *you may not be able to continue to see your regular doctors* because they aren't included in the Advantage Program's network. These choices affect your monthly costs and *which doctors you can see (called in-network healthcare professionals),* so it is worth reviewing them during Medicare's annual open enrollment period rather than assuming your current plan is still the best fit every year. Your *State Health Insurance Assistance Program*, often called SHIP, offers free, unbiased, one-on-one counseling on exactly this kind of decision and is listed in the resource directory.

Why asking before assuming pays off

Nearly every benefit covered in this book *comes with an exception, a special rule, or a nuance* that depends on your specific circumstances: your *age, your income, your spouse's specific work history, and your state of residence.* No book, including this one, can account for every combination. What this book can do is tell you *which offices to call and which questions to ask.* **This book is NOT legal guidance,** and for that you must go to the professionals in that specific area. The rest depends on a real conversation with a real person at the right agency, which is worth the time it takes, given how much it can affect your monthly income going forward.

Keeping records of your own benefits

Just as **Chapter 4** suggested a tracking sheet for the estate paperwork, keep a simple, ongoing record of your own benefits: *what you receive, from where, how much, and when it is due for review or renewal.* Some benefits require periodic redetermination, meaning you have to reconfirm your eligibility on a set schedule, and missing that deadline can cause a pause in payments even when you still qualify. A simple calendar reminder tied to each benefit's review date protects you from this kind of avoidable interruption.

A man called Gerald

A man we will call Gerald, who received both SSDI and a small pension, called a benefits counselor at his local Area Agency on Aging before making any changes at all, mostly because his late wife had always been the one who handled this kind of paperwork and he did not trust himself to get it right alone. The counselor caught something Gerald had not thought to ask about: *a small survivor portion of his wife's pension* that the pension office had not automatically added, because it required a separate form. That one phone call, made before anything else, added money to his monthly income that he otherwise would have simply gone without.

Chapter 14: Housing Decisions

Deciding whether to stay or move, without rushing

There is no deadline for deciding whether to stay in your home. In the first months, it is generally *wise to avoid large, permanent decisions* like selling a house, since grief affects judgment in ways that are hard to notice from the inside. Give yourself real time, at minimum several months, before making a decision this size.

Accessibility needs, whether you own or rent

If your home needs modifications to remain safe and workable for you, such as a ramp, grab bars, or a walk-in shower, several avenues can help with cost. Area Agencies on Aging sometimes offer home modification programs or referrals. Medicaid, in some states, covers modifications through a waiver program. Nonprofit organizations focused on aging in place or disability services, listed in the resource directory, often provide free labor or reduced-cost modifications for qualifying households. This applies whether you own your home outright or rent, though the process differs somewhat, covered below.

If you rent, not own

Everything in the rest of this chapter about deeds, titles, and mortgages applies to homeowners. If you rent an apartment or house instead, your situation is different, and it deserves its own attention here, not an assumption that you own property.

Under the federal Fair Housing Act, *a landlord generally must allow you to make reasonable modifications to your unit at your own expense if they are necessary because of a disability*, such as installing grab bars, a ramp, or lever-style door handles. The landlord cannot refuse this request outright, though they can require the work to be done properly and may require you to restore the unit to its original condition when you move out, depending on the modification.

Landlords are also *required to make reasonable accommodations* to policies or procedures, such as assigning you a parking space closer to your unit, at no cost to you, if it is needed because of a disability.

Put any request for a modification or accommodation in writing, addressed to your landlord or property manager, describing specifically what you need and why. You might also want to consider sending this certified mail so that you have an indication of when it was delivered and to whom. This creates a clear record and starts the clock on their obligation to respond. If a landlord refuses a reasonable request, you can file a complaint with the Department of Housing and Urban

Development, listed in the resource directory, which investigates Fair Housing Act violations at no cost to you.

If you live in subsidized or public housing, *the housing authority is generally required to pay for reasonable accommodations itself,* unlike a private landlord, where you typically cover the cost of a modification yourself. Ask your housing authority directly what they cover.

For renters who cannot make permanent changes to a unit, or who are not sure how long they will stay, non-permanent options are worth knowing about: portable grab bars that clamp onto a tub without drilling, a raised toilet seat, a shower chair, and portable or temporary ramps that do not require construction. Occupational therapists, sometimes available through Medicare-covered home health visits after a hospital stay or a fall, can assess your specific apartment and recommend exactly what would help most, often identifying options you would not have thought of on your own.

In-home care options and typical costs

In-home care ranges widely depending on the level of help needed, from a few hours a week of light housekeeping and companionship to full-time personal care. Costs vary significantly by region and by agency versus hiring independently. Before committing to a private-pay arrangement, *ask your Area Agency on Aging what free or subsidized in-home care options exist in your area*, since income-based programs exist in most regions and are often underused simply because people do not know to ask.

Downsizing without feeling pressured

If you do eventually decide that your current home is more than you need or can manage, downsizing is a reasonable and common choice, *but it should be your choice,* made on your timeline, not a decision pushed by a well-meaning relative or a real estate agent eager to list your house. Take your time getting more than one opinion, whether about a home's value or about your options, before committing to anything.

Property tax relief for seniors and surviving spouses

Many states and counties offer a *property tax exemption or reduction specifically for older homeowners, people with disabilities, or surviving spouses.* This is easy to miss because it usually requires filing an application rather than being applied automatically. Contact your local county assessor's office and ask directly whether you qualify for any exemption based on your age, disability, or status as a surviving spouse.

Renting out part of your home

If your home has more space than you need and moving does not appeal to you, renting out a room or an accessory unit, if you have one, is one way to bring in additional income while staying in a home you know and can navigate. This is not the right fit for everyone, particularly if privacy or accessibility concerns make it impractical, but it is worth considering as one option among several rather than dismissing it outright.

A reverse mortgage and why to be cautious

You may hear about reverse mortgages as a way to access money from your home's value without moving. These products can work for some homeowners, *but they are complicated, come with real costs and risks, including the possibility of losing the home if requirements are not met*, and are a frequent source of aggressive sales tactics aimed at older homeowners. If a reverse mortgage is suggested to you, *take it to a HUD-approved housing counselor,* which federal law requires before you can close on one anyway, and consider it a starting point for questions, not a sales pitch to accept. Remember, just because a famous movie star or entertainer is promoting reverse mortgages on television does not mean this is a good choice for you, but it also does not ensure that it won't come with some things that will cause you unknown issues in the future.

Moving closer to support, if that ever makes sense

Some widowed people, particularly those without children nearby, eventually consider moving somewhere with more built-in support: closer to a sibling or close friend, into a senior living community, or into a smaller home with less upkeep. This is a significant decision and should never be made under pressure or on a tight timeline. If you do explore this option, *visit any community in person more than once, at different times of day,* and talk directly with current residents if possible, not just staff, before deciding.

A note on accessibility when evaluating any new place

If you use a wheelchair, a walker, or otherwise need an accessible layout, *do not rely on a listing's description alone.* Visit in person, or send someone you trust to *check specific measurements*: doorway widths, step-free entry, bathroom layout, and how far parking is from the entrance. What one person calls "accessible" varies widely, and confirming it yourself avoids an unpleasant surprise after a move is already underway.

Often, doors can present the biggest problem since they may be heavy and not easily opened by someone who doesn't have strength in their arms or the use of their hands. Special automatic door openers are available on many buildings, especially those that house individuals with disabilities. Ramps and sloped entryways are also desirable, but the entryways may present problems if they receive frequent rain or where snow will accumulate.

In this era of climate change, we all need to consider how the building will incorporate fresh or air-conditioned air into it; is it individually managed in a person's apartment, or is it central air? I had an older friend who moved into a lovely apartment complex where, theoretically, the central air could be controlled in three locations in her apartment. Unfortunately, the air did not work in two of the rooms. To make the repair, the building management required a large deposit for their repairs, even though she had bought the condo.

Another building required a repair to the peephole in the apartment entry door for safety reasons. The tenant, who also had bought into the co-op, was told she would have to pay for the change. She said, "The door belongs to the building. If I leave, I don't take the door with me. It's a building requirement, and therefore you need to fix it at your expense, not mine." One woman stood up for her rights, and the other lived in an apartment where she couldn't regulate her air conditioning in two rooms.

Getting help with the physical work of a move

If you do decide to move, whether across town or into a smaller home, the physical labor of packing, sorting, and moving is often the hardest part, especially without a spouse to share the work with and without children to call on. Senior move managers are professionals who specialize in exactly this kind of transition and can handle sorting, packing, and coordinating movers for a fee. Some nonprofit and faith-based organizations also offer volunteer moving help for older adults and people with disabilities. Ask your Area Agency on Aging whether either option exists in your community before assuming you must manage a move entirely on your own.

Chapter 15: Finding Professionals You Can Trust

What an elder law attorney does, and when you need one

An elder law attorney specializes in issues that commonly affect older adults:

- probate
- wills
- powers of attorney
- long-term care planning
- benefits like Medicaid

You likely need one if your spouse's estate is *going through formal probate*, if you are updating your own estate plan, as covered in **Chapter 11**, or if you are navigating Medicaid eligibility for long-term care. Initial consultations vary widely, from free to several hundred dollars, so *ask about the cost of a first meeting before you schedule it.*

What a fee-only financial advisor does

A fee-only financial advisor is *paid directly by you, a flat fee or an hourly rate*, rather than through commissions on products they sell you. This matters because *it removes the incentive to recommend an investment or insurance product* simply because it pays the advisor more. If someone offers you financial advice for "free" and then recommends buying a specific investment or insurance product, *ask directly how they are compensated before proceeding.*

Free and low-cost help

Legal aid organizations for wills, powers of attorney, and probate questions. Nonprofit credit counseling agencies, which can help build a budget or negotiate with creditors at little or no cost, unlike for-profit debt settlement companies, which *often charge high fees.* Benefits counselors through your Area Agency on Aging, as covered in **Chapter 13.** All of these are listed by category in the resource directory in the back of this book.

Questions to ask before hiring anyone

- How are you paid, and by whom?
- What is the total cost for this specific task, and will you put it in writing?
- Can you give me two references from clients in a similar situation to mine?
- What happens if I am not satisfied with the work?

A trustworthy professional answers these questions plainly and does not pressure you to decide on the spot.

A tax preparer or accountant

A qualified tax preparer or certified public accountant can help you navigate your first tax return after your spouse's death, when filing status and income sources both change at once, as covered in **Chapter 12**. Free tax preparation help is available through AARP Tax-Aide for taxpayers of any age and through the IRS Volunteer Income Tax Assistance program for those who qualify based on income, disability, or limited English. Both are listed in the resource directory.

A geriatric care manager

If coordinating your own care, or the services covered in **Chapter 16 and Chapter 17**, feels like more than you can manage alone, a geriatric care manager, sometimes called *an aging life care professional*, is a paid specialist who can assess your needs and coordinate services on your behalf. This is a private-pay service in most cases, not typically covered by Medicare, so *ask about cost upfront,* but it can be worth it if you have no one else able to take on this coordinating role.

Checking credentials before you hire anyone

Before hiring an attorney, financial advisor, or care manager, you can generally *verify their license or credentials* through your state's bar association for attorneys, the *Financial Industry Regulatory Authority's* free *BrokerCheck* tool for financial professionals, or a national certifying body for care managers. This takes only a few minutes and is a reasonable, ordinary step, not an insult to the professional you are checking on.

Building your team gradually, not all at once

You do not need to hire every professional described in this chapter right away, or possibly ever. Most people build this kind of support gradually, adding a professional only when a specific need arises: an attorney when you actually update your will, a tax preparer when your return gets more complicated than you can manage alone, a care manager only if coordinating your own care becomes more than you want to handle by yourself. Think of this chapter as a reference to return to when a specific need comes up, not a checklist to complete all at once.

Getting a second opinion when something feels off

If a professional's advice, a fee, or a recommendation ever feels wrong to you, even if you cannot fully explain why, *it is reasonable to pause and get a second opinion* from someone else before proceeding. This applies to legal advice, financial recommendations, and care decisions alike. A good professional will not be offended by a client who wants to be sure, and if one is offended by that request, that reaction alone is useful information.

When to bring in a professional versus handling something yourself

Not every task in this book requires a professional. Reporting a death to Social Security, notifying a utility company, or updating a beneficiary form are all things most people can do on their own with the guidance in this book. A professional becomes worth the cost when the stakes are higher or the situation is more complicated than usual: a contested inheritance, a Medicaid planning question, a business your spouse owned, or a tax situation you genuinely do not understand. When in doubt, a single paid consultation to ask, "*Can I handle this myself, and if not, what would you charge,*" is often a worthwhile investment even if you ultimately decide to do the rest yourself.

PART 5: Daily Life and Care

This part addresses *the everyday reality of living alone*, especially without children nearby and with a disability to manage. You will learn where to find practical help when there is no family close by to call on, how to manage your own health care and advocate for yourself at appointments, and how to build a real support network from the ground up, made of neighbors, friends, community organizations, and paid help where it makes sense. None of this happens overnight, and none of it requires you to have all the answers today. It happens the same way most of this book does: one specific, manageable step after another.

Chapter 16: Getting Help Without Family to Call

Home health aides: finding, vetting, and affording them

A home health aide *can help with bathing, dressing, meal preparation, light housekeeping, and companionship.* You can find one through a licensed home care agency, which handles background checks and scheduling, or by hiring independently, which usually costs less but puts the vetting responsibility on you. If hiring independently, always check references and consider a basic background check, available through many online services for a modest fee. *Ask your Area Agency on Aging about subsidized in-home care programs before assuming you must pay full price out of pocket.*

Physical, hands-on help specifically

If your spouse used to physically assist you, helping you get out of bed, transfer to a wheelchair, get in and out of the shower, or move safely around your home, be direct about naming this specific kind of help when you ask for it. "*Help around the house*" is vague and easy for even a well-meaning helper to underestimate. "*I need someone who can safely help me transfer from my bed to my wheelchair every morning*" is specific enough that an agency, a caseworker, or a friend understands exactly what is being asked of them. In a large apartment complex, people who want to have a small dog as a companion but are mobility-challenged hire someone to take their dog out two or three times a day. That's all.

Home health aides and personal care aides are trained specifically for this kind of hands-on physical assistance, *unlike a general house-keeper or companion*, so be clear with an agency about which type of help you need when you call. If you were recently hospitalized or had a fall, ask your doctor about a referral for a home health evaluation, *which Medicare often covers*, including a visit from an occupational or physical therapist who can assess exactly what kind of help and equipment would make your home safer, whether you own it or rent it, as covered in **Chapter 14.**

Getting equipment, not just people

Beyond hired help, equipment alone can restore a real measure of independence: a raised toilet seat, a shower chair, a walker, a wheel-chair, or a hospital bed. Medicare and Medicaid cover many of these items, called *durable medical equipment,* when prescribed by a doctor, though rules and coverage amounts vary. Beyond insurance, many communities have a medical equipment loan closet, often run by a local Lions Club, a faith community, or a nonprofit health organization, where *used equipment is lent out or given away at no cost.* Your Area Agency on Aging or a hospital discharge planner, if you have recently been in the hospital, usually knows where the nearest one is.

Area Agencies on Aging and what they offer for free

Area Agencies on Aging exist specifically to help older adults and their caregivers find services in their own communities. Their offerings commonly include *home-delivered meals, transportation assistance, caregiver support, home modification help, and legal service referrals,* often at no cost or on a sliding scale. Reach yours through the Eldercare Locator at 1-800-677-1116 or online at eldercare.acl.gov, where you can search by ZIP code.

State and local disability services

If you receive disability benefits or live with a disability regardless of benefit status, your state's disability services office can connect you to additional support, including personal care assistance programs, equipment loans, and independent living resources. Many states also have a Center for Independent Living, a nonprofit specifically run by and for people with disabilities, which can be a valuable source of practical, peer-based advice.

Meal delivery, transportation, and other everyday supports

Meals on Wheels and similar programs deliver food directly to the home, often on a sliding scale based on income, and are available in most communities through the Area Agency on Aging network. Transportation support varies by area but commonly includes volunteer driver programs, reduced-fare paratransit for people with disabilities, and rides arranged through local senior centers. There is also another very well-known volunteer service known as FISH (standing for *Friends in Service Here or Friends in Service Helping*) that is locally administered. Primarily, they volunteer to take people to appointments or for other activities for which they need a ride.

Paying a family member or friend for care

In some cases, a friend or family member who is already helping with your care *can be formally paid* for that work through certain Medicaid programs, sometimes called consumer-directed or self-directed care programs. This turns informal help into a modest paid arrangement, which can make it more sustainable for both of you over the long term. Ask your state Medicaid office or your Area Agency on Aging whether this kind of program exists where you live.

Respite and adult day programs

If you are the one receiving care rather than only giving it, and you also worry about placing too much on a single caregiver, adult day programs offer supervised daytime activities and support outside the home, giving structure to your day and a break to anyone helping you. *Respite care provides short-term relief for a family caregiver specifically,* whether for a few hours or a few days. Both are typically arranged through your Area Agency on Aging.

Faith-based and community volunteer support

Many congregations run visitation or parish nurse programs specifically for members who are homebound, ill, or newly widowed, offering everything from friendly visits to help with errands. You do not need to belong to a congregation formally to ask whether a local one offers this kind of community support; many extend it to anyone in the surrounding neighborhood.

Vetting anyone who comes into your home

Whether you hire a home health aide independently, through an agency, or accept help from a new acquaintance, *take reasonable precautions before letting someone into your home regularly.* Ask for and check references. Consider a background check, which many online services offer for a modest fee. Trust your own instincts if something feels off, and know that it is completely acceptable to end an arrangement that is not working, regardless of how it started. One woman who had a visiting nurse service send someone to her home for post-operative wound care found that the traveling nurse was disagreeable. She called the agency and told them that she wanted someone else and that this woman was never to be sent to her home again. There was no problem, and they supplied a different nurse.

Technology that can help you stay independent

A range of simple tools can extend how long you manage comfortably on your own: *a medical alert device* you wear that connects to help at the press of a button, *automatic medication dispensers* that remind and dispense doses on schedule, and *video calling for easy contact with family, friends, or a care coordinator.* None of these are required, and none of them replace human connection, but for many people living alone, especially with a disability, they add a real layer of safety and peace of mind. Ask your Area Agency on Aging whether any subsidized programs exist locally to help cover the cost.

Otis' story

A widower we will call Otis had no children and had always let his wife manage the social side of their lives together. In the months after she died, he built what he later called his "team" almost by accident: a home health aide three mornings a week through a subsidized program his Area Agency on Aging told him about, a neighbor who mowed his lawn in exchange for Otis watching her dog on weekends, and a volunteer driver through his senior center who took him grocery shopping every other Tuesday. None of it happened at once. It took him a few months of asking one question at a time, but by the end of that first year, he was not managing alone anymore, even without a single relative living nearby.

Chapter 17: Managing Health Care Alone

Getting to appointments and advocating for yourself

If your spouse used to come to appointments with you, ask a friend or a volunteer driver, covered in **Chapter 16,** to step into that role, at least for appointments where a second set of ears is useful, such as a new diagnosis or a change in medication. If no one is available, ask the doctor's office directly whether you can *bring a phone to record notes* or whether a nurse can call a family member or friend afterward with a summary, with your permission.

A man who had recently gone through heart surgery had to have his wife receive information about the surgery, the prognosis, the treatment, et cetera. All of it would have been too much for anybody to remember. She did record all of the conversation, and her phone automatically transcribed it into text, which she could then transfer to her computer.

Keeping your own medical information organized

Keep a simple written list of your medications, dosages, allergies, and major diagnoses, and bring it to every appointment. This single habit prevents a great deal of confusion, especially if you see more than one doctor, and it means you are not relying on memory alone during a stressful appointment.

Telehealth as an option

If getting to appointments is physically difficult, ask your doctor's office whether a telehealth, or video, appointment is available for visits that do not require a hands-on exam, such as medication check-ins or follow-up discussions. Many practices expanded this option significantly in recent years, and it remains widely available, though not every type of appointment can be done this way.

Coordinating care across multiple doctors

If you see several different doctors, it helps to have one central place, whether a folder, a notebook, or a shared online patient portal, where test results and visit summaries collect in one spot, since specialists do not always automatically share information with each other. If your income and health situation qualify, a patient advocate or care coordinator, sometimes available for free through a hospital system or

Area Agency on Aging, can help manage this coordination on your behalf.

Getting help with prescription costs

If prescription costs are a strain, ask your doctor about *generic alternatives, and ask your pharmacist directly whether any manufacturer assistance programs, discount cards, or the Medicare Extra Help program* mentioned in **Chapter 13** apply to what you are taking. Pharmacists are an underused source of this kind of guidance and are usually glad to help you find a lower-cost option.

Bringing someone with you, even briefly

If a friend or volunteer driver cannot stay for an entire appointment, ask whether they can at least join for the first few minutes when the doctor explains the plan or be reachable by phone afterward for you to recap what was said. Even a short window of extra support can catch details that are easy to miss when processing new information alone. Someone coming with you can also act as an advocate or can ask questions which may not have occurred to you.

When your own disability adds another layer

If you are managing your own chronic condition or disability while also grieving, be honest with your care team about the added strain, since stress and grief can affect symptoms, sleep, and how well you manage an existing condition. This is worth naming out loud to a doctor rather than assuming they will notice on their own, since it may shape what they recommend or how closely they want to check in with you over the coming months.

Keeping your own appointments, not just urgent ones

It is common, in the middle of grief and paperwork, to let your own routine checkups and screenings slide, especially if your spouse used to be the one keeping track of them. Try to keep at least your basic annual checkups on the calendar, even if everything else feels like it deserves more attention right now. *Preventive care matters just as much now as it did before,* and catching a problem early is easier than managing one that went unnoticed for a year or more.

If you need a new primary doctor

If your spouse's death also means a change in your health insurance, as covered in **Chapter 12,** you may need to find a new primary care doctor who accepts your new coverage. Ask your insurance company for a list of doctors accepting new patients, or ask your Area Agency on Aging for a referral, and *do not hesitate to switch again if the first doctor you try is not a good fit for your needs.*

Choosing an emergency contact and a backup

Every medical form asks for an emergency contact. Choose someone reliable, and ask them directly if they are willing to serve in that role before listing their name. Choose a second backup contact as well, since a single point of contact can be unreachable at exactly the moment they are needed. If you genuinely have no one close enough to ask, some Area Agencies on Aging and community organizations offer check-in programs that can serve a similar function.

Chapter 18: Building a Support Network From Scratch

Friends, neighbors, and faith communities as practical support

A support network is not only for emotional comfort. Friends, neighbors, and members of a faith community, if you belong to one, can also provide real practical help: a ride, a hand with a repair, or someone to call when you just need to hear another voice. *Don't assume people will offer without being asked.* Most people want to help but genuinely don't know what is needed unless you tell them.

Finding a grief support group

Grief support groups, whether in person or by phone, connect you with people who understand this specific kind of loss without needing it explained. *GriefShare* runs a thirteen-week program with locations across the country, found at *griefshare.org*. *Modern Widows Club* offers community and financial assistance specifically for widows, with no one turned away for inability to pay, at *modernwidowsclub.org*. *The National Widowers' Organization* offers free resources **built specifically for men** at *nationalwidowers.org*. Full contact information for all of these is in the resource directory.

How to ask for help clearly

Asking for help gets easier with practice, and it works best when it is specific. Instead of *"I could use some help,"* try *"Could you drive me to my appointment Thursday at two?"* A specific, small ask is easier for someone to say yes to, and it is not over-explaining or apologizing to simply state what you need.

Online communities and phone-based companionship

If getting out to an in-person group is hard, online grief communities and forums, such as those run by *GriefNet* and *Soaring Spirits International*, offer connection from home, on your own schedule. *The Friendship Line,* run by the *Institute on Aging*, is a free, staffed phone line specifically for older adults who want regular, friendly phone contact, whether they are in crisis or simply looking for someone to talk to; it can be reached at 1-888-670-1360.

Volunteering as a way back into connection

When you feel ready, and there is no set timeline for when that might be, volunteering is one way some widowed people naturally rebuild a sense of purpose and community at the same time. It does not need to be a large commitment. A few hours a month at a library, a food pantry, or an organization tied to something you already care about can be enough to start. A woman I knew was a 9/11 survivor who had seen her friends die during the attack and for years afterward. The grief she felt was best handled, she believed, by going to her local food pantry and volunteering every week. After that, she also went, when approached to do so, to local schools and spoke at assemblies for young students so they would know what it was like and how she handled her grief. Both activities gave her a feeling of purpose and uplifted her spirits.

Rebuilding trust in yourself

Beyond rebuilding a support network of other people, part of this stage is rebuilding trust in your own judgment, especially if your spouse handled certain decisions for most of your marriage. It is common to feel unsure of yourself in areas you never had to manage before, whether that is finances, home repairs, or medical decisions. This uncertainty tends to ease with practice and with small successes, one decision at a time. Every chapter in this book that you have worked through is evidence, even if it does not feel that way yet, that you are capable of handling things you once assumed only your spouse could handle.

I recall a co-worker once telling me that when her father died, the family was absolutely shocked to find that their mother didn't know how to write a check and had never paid bills. To their surprise, when they opened a desk drawer in the home, they found scores of unpaid bills that the mother had just received in the mail and put in the drawer as usual when her husband was still alive. While he was there, he would go into the desk, remove the bills, make out the checks, and take them to the office to be mailed. The mother was reluctant to learn how to make out checks and felt she was utterly incapable of paying bills, but the daughters persisted gently and helped her make the transition.

It is fine for your network to look different than expected

Without children to lean on, your support network may end up being a wider, looser mix of people than a family-centered network typically looks like: a few close friends, a neighbor, a fellow group member, a paid aide who has become someone you trust, a sibling who lives far away but calls every week. There is no requirement that support come from family, or that it come from any particular number of people. What matters is *that it is real, reliable, and reachable when you need it, whatever shape it takes.*

Starting small if reaching out feels hard

If the idea of joining a group or reaching out to new people feels like too much right now, start smaller than you think you need to. A single phone call to one grief support line. One short visit to a group, with permission to leave early if it doesn't feel right. One message to a neighbor. Building a support network rarely happens in one large step. It happens through small, repeated efforts, and it is fine if progress looks slow from the inside while still adding up over time.

PART 6: Grief and Moving Forward

This part closes the book by returning to you, not just the paperwork. Everything up to this point has focused on tasks: forms, phone calls, decisions, and deadlines. This part is different. It is about the grief that has likely been sitting alongside all of that task-work the entire time, whether or not you have had a chance to fully feel it yet. It is about finding purpose again, on no particular schedule, and it closes with a plain and honest word about what comes next, because you deserve honesty here more than you deserve false comfort.

Chapter 19: Grief on Top of Everything Else

Why grief and paperwork happen at the same time

Most people expect grief to arrive quietly, with time to feel it fully. Instead, it usually arrives at the same time as death certificates, phone calls to Social Security, and decisions about a funeral bill. This is not a sign that you are doing grief wrong. It is simply the reality of what happens after a death, and it is normal, not a personal failure, to feel both heartbroken and buried in forms in the same afternoon.

Common grief reactions, explained simply

Grief does not move in a straight line, and it does not look the same for everyone. You may feel numb for a while, as if none of this is fully real yet. You may feel intense sadness that comes in waves rather than staying constant. You may feel anger at the situation, at doctors, and sometimes even at your spouse for dying. You may feel relief, especially if your spouse suffered a long illness, and then feel guilty for feeling relief. All of these are common, and none of them mean something is wrong with you.

Grief can show up in your body, not just your emotions

Grief is not only emotional. It is common to notice trouble sleeping, changes in appetite, low energy, or difficulty concentrating in the weeks and months after a loss. These physical effects are a normal part of grieving for most people and tend to ease gradually over time, though not always in a straight line.

Certain days can be harder than others

Anniversaries, holidays, a wedding date, or even an ordinary Tuesday that happened to be a routine you shared can bring grief back with unexpected intensity, even well after you thought you were doing better. This is a normal pattern, not a setback or a sign that earlier progress was undone. Some people find it helpful to plan something small and comforting on days they know will be hard, rather than being caught by surprise.

When to reach out for additional support

For most people, grief eases gradually with time, even though *it never fully disappears*. If your grief feels like it is not easing at all after many months, or if it is consistently preventing you from managing daily tasks like eating, sleeping, or basic self-care, it is worth talking to a doctor or a grief counselor, who can help you understand what you are experiencing and what additional support might help. Reaching out for this kind of help is not a sign of weakness. *It is the same kind of practical step as anything else in this book.*

Giving yourself permission to be behind

There is no schedule for grief and no schedule for the paperwork in this book that cannot bend if you need it to. If a form sits for an extra week because you needed that week to simply get through the days, that is not failure. Most deadlines in this book have more flexibility than they first appear to, and asking for an extension, from a bank, an insurance company, or a government office, is a reasonable and common request after a death in the family.

A woman we will call Coral spent an afternoon filling out survivor benefit paperwork without shedding a single tear, and she felt strange about it afterward, almost guilty, as though not crying while doing something so connected to her husband's death meant something was wrong with her. Months later, in a grief support group, she said this out loud for the first time, and several other people in the room nodded, because they had felt exactly the same thing. Grief doesn't always show up when you expect it to, and it doesn't always look like crying. Filling out a form calmly is not evidence that you didn't love someone. It is often simply what the moment required of you.

Grieving without children in the house

If you have no children or they have left to begin their own lives, there is no one else in your home experiencing this loss alongside you day-to-day, no small routines to keep up for someone else's sake, and no one to comfort in the same shared grief. This can make the house feel especially quiet, and it can also mean fewer of the built-in reasons to keep functioning that a parent of young children might describe. If this describes your situation, be especially deliberate about staying connected to people, through the support network covered in **Chapter 18,** since the structure that children might otherwise provide will need to come from somewhere else.

Managing grief while managing a disability

If you live with a disability, grief and physical symptoms can sometimes tangle together in confusing ways. Fatigue, pain, or a flare in symptoms may be harder to separate from grief's physical toll, described earlier in this chapter, and either one can worsen the other. Be patient with yourself here specifically. It is not always possible, or necessary, to know exactly which part of a hard day is grief and which part is your body, and treating yourself gently either way is a reasonable response.

Chapter 20: Finding Purpose Again

Small routines that rebuild a day

After a death, ordinary routines often disappear along with the person who shared them: a morning coffee together, a nightly walk, a weekend errand you always ran as a pair. Rebuilding small routines, even simple ones, gives shape back to a day that might otherwise feel shapeless. This does not need to be complicated. A regular time to get up, a short walk, a phone call to a friend on the same day each week. Small and steady works better than big and occasional.

Trying something new, without pressure or a deadline

At some point, often further along than you might expect right now, some people find it helpful to try something new: *a class, a volunteer role, or a hobby they never had time for before.* There is no timeline for when, or whether, this happens for you, and it is not a requirement or a sign of healing if it does not interest you. If and when it feels right, trying something small, with no pressure to stick with it, is enough.

Reconnecting with people

It is common to lose touch with some friendships during a long illness or during the early months of grief, simply because there was little energy left for anything beyond what was necessary. When you are ready, reaching back out, even with a short message after a long silence, is usually welcomed far more warmly than people expect. Most friends understand exactly why the silence happened and are glad to hear from you again.

Considering a pet

Some widowed people, especially those living alone for the first time, find real comfort in a pet's companionship and the small structure that caring for one provides, such as a regular schedule and a reason to get up and move. This is not the right choice for everyone, particularly if a disability or living situation makes pet care difficult, but it is worth considering if it has ever appealed to you. Some shelters and rescue organizations offer reduced adoption fees for older adults.

The choice of pet is particularly important, since there is a great difference between having a bird in a cage in your home and having a dog that may need to be taken out on walks, regardless of the weather or your feeling that day. Cats, of course, can be kept in the home and present less of a challenge for people in terms of weather. In fact, they present no challenge regarding weather.

Travel and new experiences, at whatever scale fits

For some people, eventually taking a trip, even a short one, marks a meaningful step forward. For others, staying close to home and routine feels better, and that is equally valid. There is no correct answer here, only the one that fits you.

Marking meaningful dates in your own way

Anniversaries, birthdays, and holidays that once revolved around your spouse do not have to disappear or be avoided entirely. Some people find comfort in marking them deliberately: lighting a candle, visiting a meaningful place, cooking a favorite meal, or simply spending the day quietly rather than pretending it is an ordinary one. Others prefer to let the day pass without ceremony. Either approach is reasonable, and it is fine for your approach to change from year to year as your grief itself changes over time.

Noticing small signs of moving forward

Progress after a loss like this rarely arrives as one clear turning point. It tends to show up in small, easy-to-miss ways: a full night's sleep, laughing without immediately feeling guilty about it, making a decision without hesitating, looking forward to something, even something small, for the first time in a while. These moments do not mean grief is over, and they are not a betrayal of your spouse's memory. They are simply signs that you are, gradually and in your own time, finding your footing again.

Chapter 21: When You're Ready

There is no timeline, and this chapter says so plainly

You may have picked up this book expecting a final chapter that tells you grief ends by a certain point, or that a certain number of months should have you feeling like yourself again. Or that there are absolute and definite stages of grief that you must go through.

No, that is not the case. Grief is highly individual, and you will go through it as you will, not as someone else said you should. This chapter will not tell you that, because it is not true. Grief changes over time for most people, often becoming less constant and less overwhelming, but it does not run on a fixed schedule, and there is no date by which you are supposed to be finished with it.

Looking ahead on your own terms

Whatever comes next in your life, whether that is staying exactly where you are for now, moving, building new routines, or reconnecting with people you had lost touch with, it can happen on your own terms and your own timing. Nobody else gets to decide when you are ready for any of it.

If new relationships come into your life someday

Some widowed people eventually welcome a new close friendship or a new romantic relationship into their lives. Others do not and never feel a pull toward that, which is equally valid. If it does happen for you, it is common to feel a mix of guilt and happiness at the same time, as though caring about someone new says something untrue about how much your spouse mattered. It does not. Loving again, in whatever form that takes, does not erase or diminish what came before it.

I recall working with a man whose mother had passed about two years previously, and his father had begun seeing a woman. When someone said something negative about the father dating now, the man turned around and said to him, "It was a wonderful marriage, and he's looking for it again."

Carrying your spouse's memory forward

Moving forward does not mean forgetting. Many widowed people find ways to carry their spouse's memory forward into their new life, whether through a small yearly tradition, a cause their spouse cared about, or simply the values and habits their spouse helped shape in them. This is not a requirement, and there is no correct way to do it. If it happens naturally, it can be a source of real comfort rather than something that holds you back.

What to do with belongings and keepsakes

There is no required timeline for sorting through your spouse's belongings, and there is no correct way to do it. Some people find it easier to do this quickly, while grief is still fresh and the task feels almost mechanical. Others need months or longer before they can face it at all. Both are normal. When you are ready, it is fine to keep some things permanently, give some things away to people who would value them, and let go of the rest, in whatever proportion feels right to you. Nobody outside your own household gets a vote in this decision unless you choose to invite one.

If you find yourself helping someone else through this later

Having gone through this yourself, you may find that you understand, in a way you could not have before, what a newly widowed friend or neighbor actually needs. If that day comes, remember what helped you: practical, specific offers of help, patience with an uneven pace, and permission to not be fine yet. You are now one of the people who understands, and that understanding, passed along to someone else someday, is its own kind of meaningful thing to carry forward.

A closing note to the reader

You picked up this book at one of the hardest points in your life, and you worked through pages of paperwork, phone calls, and decisions that no one should have to face alone, especially while grieving and especially without children to lean on. That took real strength, even on the days it did not feel like strength at all. Wherever you are right now, whether still deep in the first weeks or further down the road, you are not behind, and you are not alone in this. Go at your own pace. Ask for help when you need it. And know that the fact you are still here, still reading, still moving forward one step at a time, already says something true about you.

Checklists

These three checklists pull together the most important action steps from the chapters you have just read, organized by timeframe rather than by topic. Use them the way that works best for you: as a quick reference to make sure nothing important slipped through, as a starting point before you have read the full chapters, or simply as a way to see your progress by crossing off what is done. None of these are meant to be completed in order or all at once. Some items will not apply to your situation at all, and that is fine. Skip anything that does not fit and come back to anything you are not ready for yet.

First Week Checklist

- Call 911, or the hospice nurse line if your spouse was under hospice care.
- Choose a funeral home or cremation provider, or contact the one already on file if a plan was prepaid.
- Ask for a written, itemized price list before agreeing to any services.
- Order eight to twelve certified copies of the death certificate

through the funeral home.

- Call one or two close family members or friends to be with you or on the phone with you.
- Ask one trusted person to help spread the word to the wider circle of friends and family.
- Say yes to offers of practical help: meals, rides, or company.
- Avoid signing any contract or agreement you have not had time to read.
- Avoid making any decision about your house, car, or spouse's belongings.

First 30 Days Checklist

- Set up a simple filing system: folders or a box, sorted by topic.
- Call Social Security at 1-800-772-1213 to report the death and ask about survivor benefits.
- Contact any pension office and ask specifically about survivor benefits.
- Contact retirement account or annuity companies where you are the named beneficiary.
- File a life insurance claim if a policy exists.
- Notify the bank of any joint or individually held accounts.

- Notify credit card companies.
- Notify the mortgage company or landlord.
- Notify utility companies: electric, gas, water, phone, and internet.
- Contact the employer's human resources office if your spouse was still working.
- Contact the union or pension office, if applicable.
- If you receive SSDI or SSI, call Social Security to ask how a survivor benefit or lump sum specifically affects your benefit before spending or reporting it.

First Year Checklist

- Build a new monthly budget using actual income and expense numbers.
- Request a free benefits check-up through your Area Agency on Aging.
- Decide, without rushing, whether to stay in your home or consider other housing options.
- Update your own will.
- Name a new power of attorney and health care proxy.
- Update beneficiary forms on all of your own accounts.

- Consult a probate court clerk or legal aid office about how your state's inheritance rules apply, especially if there was no will.
- Find a grief support group, in person or by phone.
- Build a small support network of people you can call for practical help.

Resource Directory

This directory is organized by category so it stays useful no matter where you live. Where a resource is state-specific, contact the national number or website listed and ask to be connected to your local office. Phone numbers, website addresses, and program rules can change over time, so if a number in this directory no longer works, a quick internet search for the organization's name will usually lead you to its current contact information.

State Health Insurance Assistance Program (SHIP): *shiphelp.org*, or reach it through the Eldercare Locator at 1-800-677-1116. Free, unbiased, one-on-one counseling on Medicare choices, mentioned in **Chapter 13**.

Government Benefits

• Social Security Administration: 1-800-772-1213, *ssa.gov*. Report a death, apply for survivor benefits, and ask questions about SSDI, SSI, Medicare, and how they interact.

• Medicare: 1-800-MEDICARE (1-800-633-4227), *medicare.gov*.

• Medicaid: Contact your state's Medicaid office directly; a directory of state offices is available at *medicaid.gov*.

• Department of Veterans Affairs, burial benefits: 1-800-827-1000, *va.gov/burials-memorials*. Report suspected VA benefit scams to the VSAFE Fraud Hotline at 833-388-7233.

Disability Services and Aging Support

• Eldercare Locator: 1-800-677-1116, *eldercare.acl.gov*. Connects you to your local Area Agency on Aging for meals, transportation, in-home care, caregiver support, and legal referrals.

• Administration for Community Living: *acl.gov*. National information on aging and disability services and how to find local providers.

• Your state's disability services office or local Center for Independent Living: search "[your state] Center for Independent Living" or ask your Area Agency on Aging for a referral.

• U.S. Department of Housing and Urban Development, Fair Housing complaints: *hud.gov/fairhousing*, 1-800-669-9777. File a complaint if a landlord refuses a reasonable accessibility modification or accommodation, as covered in Chapter 14.

• Medical equipment loan closets: Ask your Area Agency on Aging, a hospital discharge planner, or a local Lions Club chapter about free or low-cost loaned equipment such as wheelchairs, walkers, and shower chairs.

Grief and Mental Health Support

• GriefShare: *griefshare.org*. A thirteen-week grief support program with locations nationwide.

• Modern Widows Club: *modernwidowsclub.org*. Community and financial assistance for widows; no one turned away for inability to pay.

• National Widowers' Organization: *nationalwidowers.org*. Free resources and support built for men grieving the loss of a spouse.

• Soaring Spirits International: *soaringspirits.org*. Support programs and events for widowed people of all ages, including Camp Widow.

Legal Aid and Elder Law Referrals

• Legal Services Corporation: *lsc.gov*. Directory of local legal aid offices offering free civil legal help based on income.

• *LawHelp.org*: state-by-state directory of free and low-cost legal resources.

• Eldercare Locator (1-800-677-1116) can also connect you to legal service referrals funded through the Older Americans Act for people over sixty.

• National Academy of Elder Law Attorneys: *naela.org*. Directory to help find an elder law attorney in your area.

Nonprofit Financial and Credit Counseling

• National Foundation for Credit Counseling: 1-800-388-2227, *nfcc.org*. Nonprofit, accredited credit counseling and budgeting help.

• AARP Tax-Aide: *aarp.org/taxaide*. Free tax preparation help, available to taxpayers of any age.

• IRS Volunteer Income Tax Assistance (VITA): *irs.gov*, search "VITA." Free tax preparation for qualifying households based on income, disability, or limited English proficiency.

• Consumer Financial Protection Bureau: *consumerfinance.gov* , 1-855-411-2372. Accepts complaints about mortgage companies, lenders, and other financial institutions.

Funeral, Burial, and Cremation Planning

• Neptune Society: *neptunesociety.com*, 1-800-NEPTUNE. National direct cremation provider; request a written, itemized price list before agreeing to services.

• Funeral Consumers Alliance: *funerals.org*. Independent non-profit offering unbiased information on funeral costs and consumer rights, including how to compare providers in your area.

• National Funeral Directors Association: *nfda.org*. Industry association with consumer-facing information on funeral planning and costs.

Food and Energy Assistance

• Supplemental Nutrition Assistance Program (SNAP): *fns.usda.gov/snap*, or contact your state's SNAP office directly.

• Low Income Home Energy Assistance Program (LIHEAP): *acf.hhs.gov/ocs/liheap*, or contact your state's LIHEAP office directly.

• Meals on Wheels America: *mealsonwheelsamerica.org*. Directory to find a local meal delivery program.

Fraud Reporting

• AARP Fraud Watch Network Helpline: 877-908-3360. Free guidance whether or not you are an AARP member.

• Federal Trade Commission: *reportfraud.ftc.gov*. Report scams and fraud directly to federal regulators.

• VSAFE Fraud Hotline (VA benefit scams specifically): 833-388-7233.

Additional Support

• Friendship Line, Institute on Aging: 1-888-670-1360. Free, staffed phone line for older adults seeking regular friendly contact or support.

Glossary of Terms

Beneficiary. A person named to receive money or property from an account, policy, or will.

Codicil. A written amendment to an existing will.

Death certificate. The official document proving a death occurred, including the cause and date, is needed as certified copies for most tasks in this book.

Estate. Everything a person owned at the time of death: money, property, belongings, and debts.

Executor. The person responsible for handling a deceased person's estate, named in a will or appointed by a court.

Fiduciary. Anyone legally required to act in someone else's best interest rather than their own.

Health care proxy. A person authorized to make medical decisions for someone else if they become unable to.

Intestate. The legal term for dying without a valid will.

Joint tenancy / survivorship. A form of ownership where property automatically passes to the surviving owner when one owner dies.

Letters testamentary. The court document proving an executor's legal authority to act on behalf of an estate.

Next of kin. The closest living relative, a term used mainly by hospitals and some government forms.

Payable on death (POD) / Transfer on death (TOD). A designation on a bank or investment account naming who the funds go to at death, without probate.

Power of attorney. A legal document letting one person make financial or medical decisions for another.

Probate. The court process that legally settles a person's estate after death.

Reasonable accommodation / reasonable modification. A landlord's legal obligation under the Fair Housing Act to allow a tenant with a disability to make needed physical changes to a rental unit, or to adjust a policy, at little or no cost to the tenant. Covered in Chapter 14.

Representative payee. A person or organization appointed by Social Security to manage benefit payments for someone who cannot manage them alone.

Small estate affidavit. A simplified legal form allowing property to transfer without full probate, for estates below a certain value.

SSDI. Social Security Disability Insurance, is based on work history, which can generally be combined with survivor benefits.

SSI. Supplemental Security Income, based on financial need, with strict income and resource limits.

Survivor benefit. A Social Security or pension payment made to a surviving spouse based on the deceased person's work record or plan.

Trust. A legal arrangement where property is held and managed by a trustee for the benefit of another person, often used to avoid probate.

A Final Word

Thank you for trusting this book with some of the hardest days of your life. Every chapter here was written with one goal: *to make a genuinely hard time a little more manageable*, one plain-language step at a time. You do not have to do this perfectly, and you do not have to do it alone. Take what is useful from these pages, set aside what does not apply to you, and go at whatever pace keeps you steady.

About the Author

Dr. Patricia A. Farrell is a licensed psychologist, published author of multiple self-help books and videos, an expert guest on national TV shows such as Today, The View, AC360, Court TV, MSNBC and others, a former WebMD psychologist expert/consultant, former medical consultant for Social Security Disability Determinations, National Monitor for the first medication for Alzheimer's disease and formeer psychiatric researcher at Mt. Sinai Medical Center (NYC), a senior health writer at an international major public relations firm, and an educator who has taught at the college as well as graduate and postgraduate levels; and a top health writer for Medi um.com publications. She has over four decades of experience in the field of mental health.

Dr. Farrell is a consultant to pharmaceutical firms, writes continuing education modules for mental healthcare professionals, has contributed to USMLE medical school prep courses and blogs on M edium.com and on Patreon "Dr. Farrell Unplugged," has a YouTube channel with helpful tips on multiple topics and is a biographee in Who's Who in the World, Who's Who in America and Who's Who in American Women.

A member of The American Psychological Association as well as the SAG-AFTRA union, Dr. Farrell is a former board member of the

NJ Board of Psychological Examiners, a former psychiatry preceptor at UMDNJ and a former board of directors member of Bergen Pines Hospital.

Amazon author page: https://tinyurl.com/yc3vff2n

Author book links: books2read.com/drpatriciafarrell

Booksellers: https://books2read.com/drpatriciafarrell

A Special Request

If this book has touched your heart, sparked your curiosity, or simply helped you along the way, I'd be incredibly grateful if you could take a moment to share your thoughts with a review on Amazon or wherever you discovered this book. Your words not only help other readers find books they need or enjoy, but they also mean the world to authors like me who pour their hearts into every page. Thank you for being part of this journey and for helping books find their way to the readers who need them most. It would be helpful if your review included *what book you ordered, what problem it solved and the reason you provided a review.*

Author Page on Amazon: ***https://tinyurl.com/zbrb6c9n*** and on Draft2Digital: ***https://tinyurl.com/mwta4w46***

Author Page on Draft2Digital: https://books2read.com/drpatriciafarrell

www.ingramcontent.com/pod-product-compliance
Lightning Source LLC
LaVergne TN
LVHW010725061126
851857LV00014B/1340
* 9 7 9 8 9 5 1 0 7 4 1 8 8 *